Rules to Rule

Prashant Anand is an Indian Police Service officer with extensive experience in national security, counter-insurgency, and strategic operations. Throughout his distinguished career, he has held key leadership positions across Jharkhand and other high-impact regions. He has also served with the National Investigation Agency, where he investigated terrorism-related cases and threats to internal security.

A recipient of both the Union Home Minister's Medal for Excellence in Investigation and the Police Antrik Suraksha Seva Padak, Anand brings a disciplined, systems-oriented approach to leadership. In *Rules to Rule*, his debut book, he distills timeless lessons from ancient Indian rulers into a practical guide for modern leaders.

Rules to Rule

Ancient History, Modern Lessons

Prashant Anand

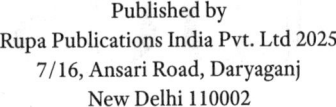

Published by
Rupa Publications India Pvt. Ltd 2025
7/16, Ansari Road, Daryaganj
New Delhi 110002

Sales centres:
Bengaluru Chennai
Hyderabad Jaipur Kathmandu
Kolkata Mumbai Prayagraj

Copyright © Prashant Anand 2025

The views and opinions expressed in this book are the author's own and the facts are as reported by him; these have been verified to the extent possible, and the publishers are not in any way liable for the same.

All rights reserved.

No part of this publication may be reproduced, transmitted,
or stored in a retrieval system, in any form or by any means,
electronic, mechanical, photocopying, recording or otherwise,
without the prior permission of the publisher.

P-ISBN: 978-93-7003-607-9
E-ISBN: 978-93-7003-505-8

First impression 2025

10 9 8 7 6 5 4 3 2 1

The moral right of the author has been asserted.

Printed in India

This book is sold subject to the condition that it shall not, by way
of trade or otherwise, be lent, resold, hired out, or otherwise circulated,
without the publisher's prior consent, in any form of binding or
cover other than that in which it is published.

*To the two wise men—my grandfathers,
Late Shri Jagannath Mishra and Late Shri Basundhar Jha*

Contents

Foreword by Prashant Kishor — *ix*
Introduction — *xiii*

1. Chandragupta Maurya — 1
2. Bindusara — 13
3. Ashoka — 20
4. Pushyamitra Shunga — 33
5. Karikala Chola — 38
6. Samudragupta — 46
7. Chandragupta II — 54
8. Prabhavatigupta — 61
9. Kanishka — 67
10. Gautamiputra Satakarni — 74
11. Harshavardhana — 82
12. Pulakeshin II — 92
13. Narasimhavarman I — 102
14. Dantidurga, Dhruva, Amoghvarsha and Krishna III — 108

15. Mayurasharma	115
16. Mihira Bhoja	122
17. Dharmapala	129
18. Rajaraja Chola	137
19. Rajendra Chola	145
Bibliography	152

Foreword

Leadership is not an abstract ideal. It is a discipline—a continuous negotiation between purpose, perception and the ability to respond to changing circumstances. Over the years, I have seen how leadership is often misunderstood as charisma or command. But in truth, it is clarity, courage and intent that shapes real leadership.

The stories in this book take us back to the political laboratories of ancient India—kingdoms and courts where leaders didn't just wield power, they built systems. From the unification of Bharat under Chandragupta Maurya to the strategic diplomacy of Harshavardhana, the vision of Rajaraja Chola, and the moral reckoning of Ashoka, each chapter brings forward a template of leadership rooted in history yet deeply relevant to our time.

We often forget that leadership—like strategy—is iterative. Improvement only comes after one realizes that they lack something and recognize the need to evolve continuously. That continuous evolution is what transformed Ashoka from a conqueror into a philosopher king. It's what drove Samudragupta to expand not just territory, but alliances. And it's what made rulers like Prabhavatigupta and Rajendra Chola invest in long-term state-building instead of short-term glory.

In a world flooded with data and noise, what distinguishes a good leader from a great one is the ability to read the moment and respond with clarity. This clarity is not incidental; it is rooted in two essential qualities: the capacity to listen—genuinely and in all its forms—and the ability to understand people not simply through metrics or electoral outcomes, but by recognizing their deeper aspirations and values.

The best rulers in this book were not just administrators. They were visionaries who governed with a sense of scale, responsibility and imagination.

Somewhere between the lines of military campaigns and royal edicts, you will find deeper lessons—on institutional thinking, decentralization, succession planning, public communication, and civilizational continuity. These are not just lessons for historians; they are cues for every modern leader, policymaker and citizen who cares about governance that lasts.

If there is one takeaway from these pages, it is that leadership cannot be inherited or imposed. Rather, it is something that each generation must earn—and continuously re-earn—through grit and persistence. And while the vocabulary of power may have changed—from thrones to offices, senates to parliaments—the fundamentals of statecraft remain remarkably consistent.

Books like this are essential not only because they tell us where we come from, but because they help us imagine where we could go—if we choose to lead with insight, not impulse.

Prashant Kishor
Founder, Jan Suraaj

Introduction

This is not a conventional history book. While it draws upon the lives and legacies of ancient Indian rulers, it is not intended as a detailed or scholarly historical account.

Instead, it is a reflection—a search for the wisdom and foresight that shaped the past, and still resonate today. It has been written for those who believe that the choices made by leaders centuries—even millennia—ago can offer valuable lessons for the present.

This book does not claim to offer shortcuts to power or guaranteed formulas for success. At best, it presents a set of time-tested 'rules'—insights distilled from the past—for those who seek to lead and sustain leadership, whether in business, politics or professional life.

But it comes with a caveat: *No rule or principle holds meaning unless it is followed in the right spirit and guided by the right purpose.*

1

Chandragupta Maurya

The Story

This is the story of a boy, raised among peacock tanners in the Vindhya Mountains, who was handpicked by Kautilya—renowned as the foremost strategist of warfare and statecraft of his time. Under his mentorship, the boy was taken to the prestigious University of Taxila for his education. Upon completing his training, he was assigned the arduous task of overthrowing the powerful Magadha kingdom. Through tactical prowess, he meticulously amassed a formidable army and eventually defeated both the Indian and Greek rulers to establish himself as one of the most influential monarchs in ancient Indian history.

> **Rules to Rule**
> - Preserve for another day
> - Volatility creates opportunity
> - Flanking is the best strategy against a centralized enemy

The Nanda Rulers

Around 400 BCE, the Shishunaga dynasty ruled Magadha, then the most powerful kingdom in ancient India. The last ruler, King Mahanandin, had two wives: Mura and Sunanda. Sunanda was involved in an illicit relationship with a barber named Ugrasen. The queen conspired with him to assassinate the king and seize the throne. Following the coup, Queen Mura fled with her young son, Chandragupta, eventually entrusting him to the headman of a peacock tanners' community in the Vindhyachal forest, where he was raised.

Meanwhile, Ugrasen, now the ruler of the kingdom, pursued an aggressive expansionist policy. He systematically subjugated the dominant Kshatriya clans, including the Maithilas, Kaseyas, Ikshvakus, Panchalas, Sursenas, Kurus, Haihayas, Vithihotras, Kalingas and Asmakas, earning him the title of 'Mahapadma Nanda'—the one who uprooted Kshatriya lineages.

Upon his death, his youngest son, Dhana Nanda, ascended the throne and presided over an empire stretching from present-day Punjab in the west to Odisha in the east. This unprecedented territorial expanse bred arrogance and excess in Dhana Nanda, culminating in his public humiliation of a visiting Brahmin scholar from Taxila. That scholar—Vishnugupta, later known as Chanakya or Kautilya—vowed vengeance and dedicated himself to overthrowing the Nanda dynasty.

Taxila was not only a centre of learning but also served as a strategic crossroad between the Indian and Persian civilizations.

Their unchecked ambition and excesses, while expanding their empire, also bred widespread discontent. It was this very arrogance and oppression that would catalyse the emergence of the empire's greatest challenger—ushered in by a humiliated scholar with a vendetta.

Chanakya's Discovery of Chandragupta

Determined to restore the rightful lineage, Chanakya set out to locate King Mahanandin's son. His search led him to the Vindhyachal forest, where he encountered Chandragupta—a boy who, while playing with his peers, instinctively assumed the role of the king in their make-believe court. Recognizing his potential, Chanakya negotiated with the village headman and took custody of the boy, bringing him to Taxila.

Located on the eastern banks of the Indus River, Taxila was not only a centre of learning but also served as a strategic crossroad between the Indian and Persian civilizations. By the time Chandragupta arrived there, Alexander III of Macedonia had already initiated his campaign to conquer the Achaemenid Empire. Chanakya, well aware of these developments, likely devised a strategy to exploit the geopolitical turbulence to Chandragupta's advantage. Under his guidance, Chandragupta was trained in statecraft, economic policy and military strategy.

The next challenge was assembling an army capable of challenging the might of Magadha. After completing his education, Chandragupta and Chanakya travelled across India, recruiting soldiers from diverse backgrounds, including the Sakas, Yavanas, Kiratas, Kambojas, Parsiks and Bahliks.

Their initial assault on Pataliputra was unsuccessful. Reportedly, during their retreat, they took refuge in the home of an old woman. Overhearing her scolding her grandson for burning his fingers while attempting to break bread from the centre—advising him instead to start from the edges—Chandragupta and Chanakya realized the flaw in their strategy. This moment inspired a tactical shift: rather than directly attacking the capital, they would first weaken Magadha's periphery.

Alexander's Campaign in India

After defeating the Achaemenid Empire, Alexander crossed the Indus and entered India through Taxila, where he faced little resistance. However, further east, he encountered King Porus, who fiercely opposed his advance. Though Porus was ultimately defeated at the Battle of Hydaspes in 326 BCE, Alexander held him in high regard and reinstated him as a satrap (governor) under Macedonian rule.

> The Nanda military boasted an army of 200,000 infantry, 20,000 cavalry, 3,000 elephants and 2,000 chariots.

Porus, recognizing the growing threat posed by Magadha, sought Alexander's assistance in subduing the Nanda kingdom. However, when Alexander's army reached the Beas River during the monsoon season, his weary troops, aware of the vast Nanda army awaiting them, refused to proceed. Facing strong resistance, Alexander was forced to retreat.

Chandragupta capitalized on the instability left in Alexander's wake. He aligned himself with Porus—a partnership that would reshape northern India's political landscape—and launched an offensive that successfully wrestled control of Punjab, the western-most province of the Nanda Empire. Employing guerrilla tactics, he systematically extended his control from Haridwar to Prayag (modern-day Allahabad), steadily increasing his resources and influence.

The Conquest of Paṭaliputra

Despite his battlefield successes, Chandragupta recognized that Pataliputra remained a formidable stronghold. At its peak, the Nanda military boasted an army of 200,000 infantry, 20,000 cavalry, 3,000 elephants and 2,000 chariots. Instead of a direct assault, he adopted a siege strategy. Chandragupta captured the surrounding cities and outposts while bribing key military officials within the Magadha army. As internal strife weakened the kingdom, the final battle ensued. Thousands perished, and King Dhana Nanda was ultimately deposed, securing Chandragupta's ascension to the throne.

Expelling the Greek Garrisons

After consolidating power in Magadha, Chandragupta turned his attention westward. In the power vacuum left by Alexander's death in 323 BCE, his generals fought for control over the empire, leaving the Greek satraps in India vulnerable. Chandragupta swiftly expelled Greek governors such as Nicanor, Philip, Eudemus and Peithon.

However, by 306 BCE—in the midst of the Wars of Alexander's Successors—one of his generals, Seleucus Nicator, had already established his authority and sought to recapture the Indian satrapies of the Macedonian Empire.

Historian John D. Grainger suggests that when Seleucus crossed the Indus River, he found himself in a precarious position, with a vast river behind and a hostile continent before him.[1]

According to Grainger, Chandragupta achieved a decisive victory, compelling Seleucus to cede significant territories west of the Indus, including Gandhara, Kandahar, the Hindukush region, and parts of Balochistan in what is now Afghanistan. The ancient Greek historian Strabo noted that Seleucus Nicator granted these regions to Chandragupta in exchange for a marriage treaty and received only 500 elephants in return. As part of the peace treaty, Seleucus sent Megasthenes as an ambassador to Chandragupta's court. This marked a significant victory for Chandragupta. The peace agreement proved mutually beneficial, keeping the Seleucid-Mauryan border stable for generations. The war elephants provided by Chandragupta also assisted Seleucus in his victory over his rival at the Battle of Ipsus.

After his victory over Seleucus Nicator, Chandragupta launched a southern campaign with an army of over 600,000 soldiers. With Chanakya's astute guidance, Chandragupta forged an alliance with the powerful Kosala kingdoms of Vadugar in Karnataka. This expansion extended his empire southwards beyond the Vindhyachal region and into the Deccan plateau.

---

[1]Grainger, John D., *Seleukos Nikator: Constructing a Hellenistic Kingdom*, Routledge, 2014, pp. 108–110.

Comprehensive Reforms and Governance

Upon ascending the throne of Magadha in 322 BCE, Chandragupta Maurya embarked on extensive reforms to establish stability and prosperity. The former ruler, King Dhana Nanda, had lost favour due to his oppressive taxation system. Recognizing this, Chandragupta and his advisor, Chanakya, implemented a uniform economic framework aimed at stimulating trade and commerce. Their taxation system was both stringent and equitable, ensuring economic stability while simultaneously cracking down on banditry along key trade routes. These reforms enhanced Chandragupta's legitimacy, strengthened his authority and facilitated economic growth.

Security and Administration

Drawing inspiration from Persian and Macedonian models, Chanakya and Chandragupta devised a decentralized governance system, dividing the empire into *janapada*s (regional administrative units).

Chanakya, as Chandragupta's chief minister, recognized the immense challenge of governing an empire of such unprecedented scale. His immediate priority was the king's safety. Assassination threats were countered with sophisticated security measures, including the employment of female bodyguards, who were considered more reliable and less susceptible to political conspiracies.

With Chandragupta's safety assured, administrative efficiency became the next focus. Drawing inspiration from Persian and Macedonian models, Chanakya and Chandragupta devised a decentralized governance system, dividing the empire into *janapada*s (regional administrative units). These territorial units were fortified with strategically positioned strongholds to maintain control. Notable capitals included Taxila for Uttarapath, Ujjain for Avanti, Toshali for Kalinga and Pataliputra for Prathya.

Infrastructure and Connectivity

Knowing the importance of connectivity for security and trade, Chandragupta embarked on an ambitious road-building initiative. According to historian Kaushik Roy, the Mauryan dynasty was instrumental in constructing extensive road networks.[2] Greek ambassador Megasthenes documented Chandragupta's construction of a thousand-mile-long highway connecting Pataliputra in Bihar to Taxila in the north-west. Additional roads linked Pataliputra to key locations such as Kapilavastu (Nepal), Dehradun (present-day Uttarakhand), Mirzapur (West Bengal), Karnataka and Odisha, enhancing both governance and commerce.

---

[2]Roy, Kaushik, *Hinduism and the Ethics of Warfare in South Asia: From Antiquity to the Present*, Cambridge University Press, 2012, pp. 62–63.

Intelligence and Internal Security

Chanakya also emphasized internal security through an advanced intelligence network. As described in the *Arthashastra*, the police department included a specialized intelligence division. Agents, known as *guptachars*, were categorized into two types: *sansthans* (stationary agents), stationed at strategic locations, and *sancharans* (roving agents), who travelled to gather intelligence. Women played an active role in espionage, further diversifying the empire's intelligence-gathering mechanisms.

Chandragupta's Spiritual Transformation

Despite his military and administrative achievements, Chandragupta's ambitions extended beyond worldly rule. Eight years after his decisive victory over Seleucus Nicator on the banks of the Indus, he embraced Jainism, seeking spiritual enlightenment.

Jain texts describe a transformative experience where Chandragupta witnessed 16 prophetic dreams on a full moon night in Kartik. Acharya Bhadrabahu interpreted these visions as forewarnings of future hardships. Under Bhadrabahu's guidance, Chandragupta abdicated the throne, passing power to his son, Bindusara. He then retreated to Shravanabelagola near Mysore, where he undertook *Sallekhana* (ritual fasting unto death), marking the final chapter of his extraordinary life.

Rules to Rule

- **Preserve for another day**
  Chandragupta's life began with retreat. After the palace coup, Queen Mura chose flight over resistance, preserving her son's life for a battle yet to come. Years later, Chanakya—publicly humiliated by the Nandas—did not react impulsively. Instead, he withdrew, planned, and returned with a vengeance that reshaped the subcontinent. True strength lies not in immediate retaliation but in knowing when to wait. Power often belongs to those who choose their moment.

- **Volatility creates opportunity**
  The north-western frontier of India trembled under Alexander's invasion. While others saw only chaos, Chanakya saw a chance. The ensuing fragmentation allowed him to move swiftly, gathering allies and building momentum. In moments of upheaval, new paths emerge. The wise do not fear instability—they harness it, turning disorder into a ladder.

- **Flanking is the best strategy against a centralized enemy**
  When the first assault on Pataliputra failed, Chandragupta did not persist with brute force. A lesson overheard in a humble village—about eating from the edges rather than the centre—revealed a

deeper truth. He turned to the periphery, chipping away at the Nanda empire piece by piece until the core collapsed. When faced with overwhelming strength, indirect routes often lead to decisive victory.

2

Bindusara

The Story

This is the story of a son whose mother tragically lost her life during his birth due to a poison that was meant for his legendary father, Chandragupta. Raised without his mother's nurturing love and amid the challenges of Pataliputra, this prince defied the odds and safeguarded the vast kingdom built by his father.

Rules to Rule

- Sometimes, quick and decisive action is essential
- After a period of growth, fatigue and disintegration are inevitable
- Not all choices can be fulfilled; destiny plays a role

Born with a Drop of Poison

In the previous chapter, we discussed the story of Chandragupta, who overthrew the Nanda ruler of Magadha and established the Mauryan Empire. However, Pataliputra proved to be a hostile environment for the new king. The city was rife with conspiracies, with assassination being the quickest route to power.

During this era, one common method of assassination was through poison girls, known as *vishkanya*s. These women were believed to seduce their targets and administer poison through food or drink. Concerned for the king's safety, Chanakya devised extensive security measures and even introduced a radical strategy: he gradually exposed Chandragupta to small amounts of poison to build his immunity.

Tragically, this plan had unforeseen consequences. One day, Queen Durdhara, Chandragupta's wife, and daughter of the defeated Nanda king Dhana Nanda, accidentally consumed poisoned food meant for her husband. She was in the final days of her pregnancy, and the poisoning proved fatal. As she lay dying, Chanakya made a decisive and ruthless choice: he ordered an emergency surgical delivery, cutting open the queen's belly to save the unborn child. The baby, born amidst this tragedy, was named Bindusara—a name symbolizing the drop of poison that marked his birth (*bindu* in Sanskrit means 'drop').

This tragedy left a deep void in Chandragupta's

personal life, even as he continued to rule. But greater challenges loomed—not just within the palace, but across the empire itself.

Confronting Challenges after Chandragupta's Abdication

Around 300 BCE, during a prolonged famine in the Mauryan Empire, Chandragupta experienced 16 prophetic dreams on a full moon night in the month of Kartik. To interpret their significance, he consulted Bhadrabahu, a revered Jain ascetic, who predicted 12 years of death and famine.

Following Bhadrabahu's guidance, Chandragupta decided to renounce his throne and embrace Jain asceticism. He migrated to Shravanabelagola with a group of Jain monks. In doing so, he abdicated the empire to his 22-year-old son, Bindusara.

Bindusara inherited an empire in turmoil. The prolonged famine had drained state revenues, religious divisions had deepened within the Jain *sangha*, and the south-eastern region of Kalinga was growing increasingly hostile. Revolts were erupting in distant provinces. However, with Chanakya continuing as chief minister, Bindusara, though young, tackled these challenges with resolve.

First and foremost, he swiftly crushed multiple revolts, earning the title 'Amrit Ghata' (slayer of rebellions).

> The southern rulers accepted Mauryan authority through persuasion rather than war.

Simultaneously, he expanded the empire's influence in the south, bringing the Chera, Chola and Satyaputra regions under Mauryan suzerainty. Rather than ruling them directly, Bindusara adopted a diplomatic approach that allowed local rulers to retain autonomy while acknowledging Mauryan supremacy. Sangam literature describes Mauryan chariots with white banners traversing southern lands, yet there is no mention of major battles—suggesting the southern rulers accepted Mauryan authority through persuasion rather than war.

On the north-western front, Bindusara maintained peaceful relations with the Seleucid Empire. He upheld his father's treaty with Seleucus Nicator and developed cordial ties with Antiochus I, the Seleucid king of Syria. In a notable exchange, Bindusara requested wine, dried figs and a sophist (Greek philosopher). While Antiochus sent the figs and wine, he humorously declined to send a sophist, stating that Greek philosophers were not for export. However, he did appoint Deimachus as his ambassador to the Mauryan court, replacing Megasthenes.

Beyond military and diplomatic efforts, Bindusara continued his father's infrastructure projects. He oversaw the completion of reservoirs, irrigation networks

> Unlike his father, who voluntarily abdicated, Bindusara remained king until his death.

and roads to strengthen trade and agriculture across the empire.

The Dispute for Succession

Unlike his father, who voluntarily abdicated, Bindusara remained king until his death. However, his final years were marred by a fierce succession struggle between his sons, Susima and Ashoka.

As part of their training, Bindusara had appointed Susima as the governor of Taxila and Ashoka as the governor of Ujjain. These assignments were meant to give them administrative experience and keep them engaged in provincial affairs. However, the rivalry between the two was already beginning to surface, as both sensed the crown would not pass quietly.

The situation escalated when a major revolt broke out in Taxila. Due to administrative misconduct, the people of Taxila rose against their governor, Susima. Unable to control the situation, he sought military assistance from the court. Instead of sending reinforcements under Susima, Bindusara dispatched Ashoka to quell the rebellion. Ashoka successfully restored order, earning admiration among ministers and officials.

This triumph shifted the balance of power in Ashoka's favour, as many in the Mauryan court began advocating for his succession over Susima. However, Bindusara remained steadfast in his preference for his elder son.

On his deathbed, he resisted ministerial pressure to name Ashoka as heir, but he could not control events beyond that point. After Bindusara's death in 274 BCE, Ashoka seized power and declared himself king.

Hearing of his father's death, Susima rushed to Pataliputra to claim the throne. However, Ashoka had already solidified his position by then. Susima was lured into a trap and pushed into a pit of burning coal, where he met a gruesome end. With this, Ashoka ascended to the Mauryan throne, marking the beginning of a transformative era in Indian history.

Rules to Rule

- **Sometimes, quick and decisive action is essential**
  When Queen Durdhara lay dying from poison, Chanakya made a decision that would haunt any mind not steeled by purpose—he ordered her womb cut open to save the unborn child. That act of resolve gave the empire a future. The hardest decisions often demand the clearest conviction, and sometimes a leader must act before certainty can offer its comfort.

- **After a period of growth, fatigue and disintegration are inevitable**
  Bindusara inherited a mighty empire, but also the strain that came with it—famine, revolt, discontent. He did not chase new conquests blindly. Instead, he strengthened the roots of the empire, securing its

borders, repairing its infrastructure and preserving its unity through diplomacy. Growth cannot endure without renewal. The wise ruler knows when to build and when to bind.

- **Not all choices can be fulfilled; destiny plays a role**
Bindusara tried to shape succession according to his will, favouring his elder son, Susima. But history is seldom obedient. Despite the emperor's wishes, Ashoka emerged from the shadows, his ascent written in a script none could revise. Sometimes, power slips from even the strongest grip—not through weakness, but because destiny's path is indifferent to plans. Even kings must bow to time, fatigue and fate.

3

Ashoka

The Story

This is the story of the greatest king in Indian history, known as 'Devnampriya'—beloved of the gods. Ashoka was rejected by his own father due to his pumpkin-like face, dark complexion and rough skin. In the early years of his reign, he fought fierce battles and decisively defeated his adversaries. But after the Battle of Kalinga, his heart changed. Compassion flowed from him, not only for men and women but also for the animals and birds that lived under his care. On his deathbed, he gave away the entire earth to the Buddhist sangha.

Rules to Rule

- What truly matters is not appearance but strength of character

> - The right person needs to step into power at the right time
> - Idealism survives only where realism is not abandoned

Not the Favourite Son

Ashoka was not the favourite son of King Bindusara. His birth story traces back to Bindusara's visit to Champa, the capital of Anga Mahajanapada, an important centre for trade and commerce. It was a bustling hub from where merchants conducted trade with various parts of the country, even the distant Suvarnabhumi in Southeast Asia. During his visit, Bindusara was captivated by a beautiful Brahmin girl named Subhadrangi, who had been prophesied by unknown fortune tellers to marry a king. Subhadrangi was brought to the capital city of Pataliputra to join the other wives in the king's palace. Out of jealousy towards her beauty, the other wives conspired to keep her away from the king. Eventually, this plot was foiled, and she gave birth to a son. This newborn boy was named Ashoka, as his mother had joyfully exclaimed, 'I am now without sorrow.'

Ashoka was born with a pumpkin-like face. His skin was

> Ashoka proved himself in Ujjain by not only quelling uprisings but also extending Mauryan control deeper into the Deccan, completing a conquest his grandfather Chandragupta had begun.

dark, rough and unpleasant to touch. Bindusara was not impressed with this son. Queen Subhadrangi's ordinary family background added to the adversities, and therefore, Ashoka was paid less attention in the backrooms of the Mauryan court. His father preferred Susima, Ashoka's stepbrother, to become the heir apparent of the kingdom and appointed him as governor of Taxila, the most important city in the empire. Meanwhile, Ashoka was sent to Ujjain, the capital of Avanti province, where the Mauryan Empire repeatedly faced conflicts with the local tribal chieftains who aspired for autonomy.

Consolidation of Mauryan Authority in Ujjain and Taxila

Ashoka proved himself in Ujjain by not only quelling uprisings but also extending Mauryan control deeper into the Deccan, completing a conquest his grandfather Chandragupta had begun. Consequently, his reputation grew in the royal court.

Around 287 BCE, a revolt broke out in Taxila due to the corrupt rule of Susima's officers. The region was too important to lose. Ashoka was sent to restore order. He marched in with a powerful force—infantry, cavalry, elephants and chariots—and forced the rebels to surrender. Ashoka's success earned admiration, especially from Radha Gupta, the prime minister and grandson of Chanakya.

The War of Kalinga

In the early years of Ashoka's reign, his court was populated by Brahmins, with Radha Gupta serving as his chief minister. Radha Gupta adhered to a philosophy of political realism. Therefore, their agenda extended beyond merely securing the throne and suppressing potential challengers. The next objective was to subdue external adversaries and command the trade routes to generate prosperity for the empire. Their initial target was the kingdom of Kalinga.

Situated between the Subarnarekha and Godavari rivers, Kalinga had become a region of ambition and prosperity after the fall of the Nanda dynasty. Its provincial ruler had asserted independence from Pataliputra amid the prevailing chaos. With fertile lands and control over vital sea routes for trade with Malay, Java and Ceylon, the region grew ambitious and eventually hostile. It began to disrupt Mauryan trade and commerce with the southern and peninsular regions of India. In response, in the ninth year of his rule, Ashoka decided to use the full might of the Mauryan Empire to quell this troublesome adversary.

Leading a vast Mauryan army himself, Ashoka engaged in a devastating war. The conflict resulted in the capture of 150,000 individuals and the death of over 100,000 people. Ultimately, Kalinga was defeated. Following the victory, a governor was appointed to oversee local affairs in the capital Toshali, and Ashoka commenced his journey back to the capital, Pataliputra.

The Great Remorse and Redemption

Ashoka's return from Kalinga was a heart-wrenching journey. The entire area was strewn with corpses and resounded with the cries of wounded soldiers. On his path, orphaned children and widows mourned the loss of their loved ones. Witnessing such extensive destruction filled Ashoka with remorse. On Major Rock Edict 13, located in the Dhauli hills in Odisha, it states:

> Nearly two years after the Kalinga war, Ashoka undertook a transformative journey to Bodh Gaya, the sacred site where Gautam Buddha had attained enlightenment.

> When he had been consecrated for eight years, the beloved of gods, the king Piyadassi, conquered Kalinga. A hundred and fifty thousand people were killed and many times that number perished. Afterwards now that Kalinga was annexed, the beloved of gods very earnestly practiced Dhamma, desired Dhamma, and taught Dhamma...[3]

After the Kalinga war, Ashoka's path to Buddhism was not a sudden conversion but a gradual transformation.

---

[3]Thapar, Romila, *Asoka and the decline of the Mauryas*, Oxford University Press, 1997, p. 255.

He met a young Buddhist monk named Nigrodh, who impressed him with his tranquil and fearless demeanour. This encounter led him to the Kukkutārāma shrine, where he met the monk Moggaliputta Tissa. Already burdened with remorse for the violence of the Kalinga war, Ashoka found solace in the principles of righteous conduct, ahimsa (non-violence), and the renunciation of war espoused by Buddhism. Over a span of two and a half years, during which he regularly interacted with the sangha (Buddhist monastic community) and Buddhist monks, Ashoka gradually embraced Buddhism.

Nearly two years after the Kalinga war, Ashoka undertook a transformative journey to Bodh Gaya, the sacred site where Gautam Buddha had attained enlightenment. There he constructed a diamond throne, known as the Vajrasana, beneath the Bodhi tree—the very spot where Buddha had achieved enlightenment. This significant location was encircled by an open pillar temple.

After this pivotal visit, Ashoka shifted from his 'Vihara Yatras' (pleasure hunting tours) to 'Dhamma Yatras'. Ashoka's commitment to Buddhism grew steadily year by year, primarily through his extensive travels to various Buddhist holy sites. During these journeys, he erected stupas and *vihara*s in memory of Gautam Buddha and regularly engaged in discussions about Dhamma—the teachings and moral principles of Buddhism—with people in rural areas. Ashoka also sought the wisdom of Brahmins, shamans and elderly individuals, presenting them with

In Ashoka's vision of Dhamma, he emphasized respect for the beliefs of others and sought to create harmony among people of different faiths. gifts of gold and valuable items.

He directed his officials to visit rural areas and promote the principles of Dhamma. Interestingly, Ashoka rarely made direct references to Buddhism in his rock and pillar edicts, which were inscribed on enduring stones. The Dhamma he emphasized was more of a moral code than a religious system. He avoided discussing metaphysical doctrines and refrained from mentioning key Buddhist concepts such as the explanation of *dukkha* (suffering), the Eightfold Path (*Astang Siddhant*), the doctrine of impermanence, or the goal of *nibbana* (nirvana).

Practised What He Preached

Ashoka's preaching was always aligned with the actions he took in his personal life. He practised what he preached, and this was evident in various aspects of his rule. For instance, when he advocated for ahimsa (non-violence) and the protection of animals, he not only renounced hunting but also abolished the royal hunting reserve. He encouraged vegetarianism and promoted the welfare of animals. He established hospitals for both humans and animals, emphasizing the importance of compassion for all living beings.

Ashoka's commitment to the welfare of his subjects was demonstrated through the construction of rest houses, wells and tree plantations along the roads. These measures aimed to provide comfort and sustenance to travellers, whether human or animal. His call for self-control, ethical conduct and tolerance of other religions mirrored his own transformation and commitment to the principles of Dhamma.

In Ashoka's vision of Dhamma, he emphasized respect for the beliefs of others and sought to create harmony among people of different faiths. He promoted courtesy, obedience to parents, generosity, and respect for elders and religious leaders. His actions and edicts reflected his genuine dedication to creating a just and compassionate society.

King Ashoka's sense of responsibility and care for the citizens of his empire indeed set a remarkable precedent in history. His proclamation stating 'all men are my children' and his desire for their prosperity and happiness, both in this world and the next, were a testament to his deep commitment to the welfare of his people. He made extraordinary efforts to stay informed about public affairs, ensuring that reports and updates on governance reached him at all hours and in various locations.

This level of accessibility and commitment to governance was unprecedented, as Ashoka's dedication to his subjects was unwavering. His emphasis on public welfare, social harmony and ethical conduct left an indelible mark on the history of leadership and governance.

Ashoka's reign stands as a shining example of a ruler who prioritized the well-being and happiness of his people above all else.

The Third Buddhist Council

Ashoka's generous patronage of Buddhism attracted followers with various philosophical views, some of which deviated from the orthodox Buddhist teachings. This led to significant disagreements between orthodox and heterodox members within the Buddhist monasteries. In response, Moggaliputta Tissa, the venerable monk who had been Ashoka's mentor in Buddhism, refused to conduct the Buddhist day of observance, known as *Uposatha*, at the Kukkutārāma monastery near Pataliputra. Instead, he withdrew to the Ahoganga Mountain for solitary retreat.

In light of this division and the need to restore unity and orthodoxy in Buddhism, Ashoka convened a great Buddhist council, the third since the death of the Buddha. Its purpose was to reorganize the Buddhist sangha and eliminate certain unacceptable practices. Moggaliputta Tissa, at Ashoka's request, presided over the council, which consisted of 1,000 monks. They gathered to recite and reaffirm the Dhamma and *Vinaya* (monastic rules).

During the nine-month-long deliberations, various philosophical and doctrinal topics were discussed, such as the existence of a personal entity, knowledge, doubts of *Arhat*s (enlightened beings), powers, emancipation, salvation, classification of things, diverse destinies, and concepts related to time, cessation and consciousness. As a result of these discussions, several monks and nuns who had violated monastic discipline were expelled from the sangha. This council played a vital role in reestablishing orthodoxy and unity within Buddhism during Ashoka's reign.

After the Third Buddhist Council, Ashoka diligently worked to implement the visionary concept of *Chakkavati Dhammiko Dharmaraja*. This concept depicted an ideal king who establishes his authority over the four quarters of the world through righteousness, avoiding violence or coercion. His sovereignty is acknowledged by all his rivals because it is not based on territorial dominance but on the ideological supremacy of Dhamma.

'Dhamma Vijay', or the victory of Dhamma, was achieved over various regions and peoples, including the Yavanas, Kambojas, Nabhakas, Nabhapanktis, Bhojas, Pitinikas, Andhras, Pilindas, Cholas and Pandyas. Ashoka also sent envoys to regions beyond the Indian subcontinent. His message of Buddha reached the dominions of rulers such as Antiochus II, the king of Syria and West Asia, Ptolemy II Philadelphus of Egypt, Magas of Cyrene in North Africa, Antigonus Gonatas of Macedonia, and Alexander of Epirus or Corinth.

Ashoka even dispatched his own children—son Mahendra and daughter Sanghamitra—to propagate the principles of Dhamma in Ceylon (Sri Lanka). When his daughter Sanghamitra was preparing to depart for Ceylon with a branch of the Bodhi tree, King Ashoka personally travelled to the ancient port of Tamralipta to bid her farewell.

Donated the Whole World to Sangha

Ashoka indeed made a remarkable effort, ahead of his time, to exert influence over a vast portion of the world through the sheer power of morality. This endeavour mirrors the concept of soft power in today's international politics. However, it is also true that he began to lose his grip on power in his later years. With none of his sons available or suitable enough to succeed him on the illustrious Mauryan throne, the search for a successor shifted to his many grandsons. This succession dispute sparked internal conflicts and diminished the king's focus on the empire's prosperity.

> On his deathbed, he asked his minister, Radha Gupta, 'Who owns the world?' Radha Gupta fell at his master's feet and replied, 'You do, my lord.' Ashoka then declared, 'I then donate the whole world to the sangha,' and passed away.

There is an intriguing tale of King Ashoka donating everything to the Buddhist sangha. When his ministers denied him access to the treasury, he donated the gold utensils that were in use. Subsequently, when the ministers replaced the gold dinnerware with silver dinnerware, those were donated as well. Finally, Ashoka began donating his own personal items, including clothes, jewels and food.

On his deathbed, he asked his minister, Radha Gupta, 'Who owns the world?' Radha Gupta fell at his master's feet and replied, 'You do, my lord.' Ashoka then declared, 'I then donate the whole world to the sangha,' and passed away.

Rules to Rule

- **What truly matters is not appearance but strength of character**
  Ashoka's story establishes the fact that while appearances can be deceiving and superficial, the strength of a person's character is what truly matters. Despite being initially disliked by his father for his physical features, Ashoka later proved his worth with qualities expected of a prince. He possessed administrative skills, valour and the unwavering determination to consolidate the position of the Mauryan Empire. When trouble arose in Taxila, a province ruled by Bindusara's favourite prince, Ashoka was dispatched to quell the revolts. After this event, the ministers of the emperor's court also realized that he would be the better ruler to serve the interests of the Mauryan Empire.

- **The right person needs to step into power at the right time**

  It is certainly to the advantage of everyone involved when the most suitable individual assumes authority at the most opportune moment. If someone less competent takes on a position of power, it can result in notably contrasting and potentially unfavourable consequences for the entire populace. The effectiveness and appropriateness of leaders can have a profound influence on the prosperity and achievements of a society. In accordance with modern values, one might not condone the way Ashoka and Radha Gupta conspired to eliminate Susima by orchestrating his fall into the coal-fire pit. Nevertheless, based on historical facts, it becomes apparent that Ashoka was the more capable candidate for the throne and he elevated the Mauryan Empire to its greatest heights.

- **Idealism survives only where realism is not abandoned**

  Idealism undeniably inspires us to strive for a better world and envision a future where humanity reaches its full potential. However, addressing the complexities of the real world and overcoming numerous challenges necessitate a thorough consideration of practical realities. Thus, idealism can only endure when rooted in a realistic perspective.

4

Pushyamitra Shunga

The Story

This is the tale of a military general who assumed power amid political turmoil to safeguard his country from external threats.

> ### Rules to Rule
> - A weak and inattentive king is often overthrown by his own general

A Failed Inspection

Fifty years after the death of King Ashoka, Brihadratha ascended to the Mauryan throne. By this time, the once-mighty empire had

Despite seizing power, Pushyamitra never took the title of king, instead continuing to be addressed as 'Senapati'...

been significantly weakened, with numerous provinces declaring independence. Even the authority of the capital, Pataliputra, was challenged. Brihadratha found himself in a helpless position, lacking both the political mandate and military strength to prevent the empire's disintegration.

To compound his troubles, the Greek-Bactrian king Demetrius was advancing towards Pataliputra with his Yavana armies. Alarmed, Brihadratha summoned his military general, Pushyamitra Shunga, expressing his desire to inspect the army. However, the ill-prepared and ineffective king was not permitted to complete this inspection. In a dramatic turn of events, Pushyamitra assassinated him in broad daylight before the assembled troops. Remarkably, no resistance followed this regicide, and Pushyamitra assumed control of the empire.

Despite seizing power, Pushyamitra never took the title of king, instead continuing to be addressed as 'Senapati', underscoring his identity as a military leader. His reign was marked by constant warfare, leaving little time for formal consecration. To reassert sovereignty over the fragmented Mauryan satraps, he conducted two *Rajasuya Yagna*s. The Rajasuya Yagna was a grand sacrifice (or *yagna*) conducted by a *chakravarti samrat* (a universal monarch) during his coronation, symbolizing his absolute sovereignty, with the participation of tributary kings.

Military Campaigns and Governance

Pushyamitra embarked on military campaigns against his southern neighbours in the Deccan and fought Kalinga in the southeast. His reign saw the defeat of the Yavana army led by King Demetrius.

Decline after the Death of Sujyestha

The first three rulers of the Shunga dynasty—Pushyamitra, Agnimitra and Sujyestha—prioritized military affairs, a stark contrast to the post-Kalinga War Mauryan rulers, who leaned toward pacifism.

Under the Shungas, the practice of sending princes on religious missions was replaced with military expeditions, emphasizing territorial defence. The Shungas reinstated Brahminical traditions, compiled the Manusmriti, and promoted the worship of Kartikeya, the warrior deity. The Shunga rulers extended acceptance to various outsiders, including the Yavanas, within the *chatur-varna* (caste system) tradition of the religion.

Despite this military focus, the Shunga rulers were not entirely dismissive of Buddhism. They repaired and maintained several Buddhist stupas and viharas originally constructed during the Mauryan period. This era also witnessed a flourishing of Sanskrit literature, notably the *Mahabhasya*, Patanjali's celebrated commentary on Panini's *Ashtadhyayi*.

After Sujyestha's death, Sumitra ascended the throne but proved unfit to govern. Unlike his predecessors, Sumitra was more inclined towards music and dance than military affairs. His inattentiveness cost him his life—he was assassinated by Muldeo, the ruler of Kosala, during a music ceremony.

Subsequent rulers, Vajramitra (nine years) and Bhagavat (32 years), saw their domain shrink as states like Kaushal, Panchal, Kaushambi and Mathura broke away. These rulers failed to mount an effective defence of their territories.

The final Shunga ruler, Devabhuti, became infamous for his preoccupation with luxury and women. His downfall came when his minister, Vasudeva, conspired to have him murdered by the daughter of a concubine. With Devabhuti's death, the Shunga dynasty ended, and Vasudeva established the Kanva dynasty.

Rules to Rule

- **A weak and inattentive king gets overthrown by his general**
  Throughout history, weak rulers have often been deposed by their own military leaders. The underlying cause is usually the same—the ruler's failure to anticipate and address impending threats. In such cases, ambitious subordinates rally support to replace the ineffective monarch, often justifying their actions

in the name of national security. The principle holds true even today—when those in charge lose focus or fail to act, others often rise to fill the void, reshaping the balance of power.

5

Karikala Chola

The Story

This is the story of the Chola king of the ancient Tamil country who faced the ordeal of being cast into flames by his enemies. Although he managed to survive, his legs got scorched. After this incident, he captured 11 royal drums—which symbolized power—from rival kings who had come to challenge him. Through this feat, he solidified the authority of the Chola kingdom, which endured in one form or another for over a millennium.

Rules to Rule

- Courage may win you the throne, but only economic foresight can help you keep it
- A leader cannot afford to be indecisive when his people are in distress

The Ancient Tamil Country

The ancient Tamil country, known as Tamilakam, witnessed a power struggle among three prominent ruling houses: Pandya, Chola and Chera. Their fierce battles aimed to establish dominance in the southern region of the Indian subcontinent. The Pandya rulers controlled the southern-most territory, Chera chieftains governed the southwestern coast of Tamilakam, while the Chola kings held sway over the eastern coast of South India and Sri Lanka. The Chola capital was Uraiyur and their royal emblem was the tiger. They claimed descent from the Suryavanshi king Shibi, who famously offered his own flesh to an eagle to protect a pigeon.

Among the early Chola dynasty rulers, Karikala stands out as one of the greatest kings, and his name is intertwined with a legend found in Sangam literature.

According to the Sangam text *Poruṇarāṟṟuppaṭai*, King Ilamcetcenni of Uraiyur (Tiruchirappalli) married a Velir princess from Azhundur who later gave birth to Karikala. Unfortunately, King Ilamcetcenni died soon after. Karikala, being of tender age, was overlooked in the line of succession, resulting in political upheaval in the kingdom. Consequently, Karikala was forced into exile. When the political

It is said that during his escape from the flames, Karikala's leg got scorched, giving rise to his name, which means 'the man with the charred leg'.

situation stabilized, Chola ministers dispatched a royal elephant in search of the exiled prince. The elephant eventually located Karikala hiding in Karuvur, modern-day Karur in Tamil Nadu. His political adversaries apprehended and imprisoned him, setting fire to the prison one night. Miraculously, Karikala managed to escape the inferno with the assistance of his uncle Irum-pitar-thalaiyan and went on to defeat his enemies. It is said that during his escape from the flames, Karikala's leg got scorched, giving rise to his name, which means 'the man with the charred leg'.

Battle of Venni

After escaping the plot orchestrated by his adversaries, Karikala successfully navigated the challenge posed by rival claimants to the Chola throne and consolidated his rule over the territory. He also strengthened the Chola army to deter potential attacks from the Pandya and Chera kings. When a coalition of the two neighbouring kingdoms and their allies sought to invade Chola territory, Karikala displayed exceptional statesmanship and secured a resounding victory at the Battle of Venni. From the rulers who had gathered to defeat him, he captured 11 royal drums.

In ancient Tamil history, particularly during the Sangam era, the number of royal drums a king seized was a measure of his military success and dominance over rival rulers. Drums (referred to as *murasu* in Tamil) were symbols of royal authority and were used in war, processions and proclamations. Karikala's capture of 11 royal drums signified that he had defeated and subjugated 11 rival kings or chieftains.

It was at the Battle of Venni that the Chera king Udyanjeral sustained a back injury, suggesting that he was wounded while trying to escape from the battlefield. This brought disgrace to the renowned ruler who, being unable to bear the shame, eventually committed suicide by slow starvation.

Following the battle, Karikala further strengthened his army to confront numerous rival chieftains. He achieved another significant victory at the Battle of Vakaipparandalai, where he defeated a confederacy of nine major chieftains and seized their umbrellas, another symbol of royal power. Subsequently, he conquered the Singhalese kingdom, extending Chola dominion over the entirety of Ceylon. The prisoners of the Singhalese war were conscripted to construct the grand Kallanai dam across the Kaveri River in the Trichy district of Tamil Nadu.

> It is said that at the time of the Kallanai dam's construction, it irrigated 69,000 acres of land, transforming Tanjore into the rice bowl of South India.

Bringing Prosperity to the Kingdom

Karikala was not just a man of great valour, who defeated almost all his rivals and gained control over a wide area between the east and west coasts. He was also a visionary who brought prosperity to his kingdom. He understood the importance of diverting water to control floods and support irrigation in the Kaveri delta region, which has always been fertile but was often troubled by severe floods during the rainy season. With the construction of the grand *anicut*, he changed the fate of the people residing in the delta region. It is said that at the time of the Kallanai dam's construction, it irrigated 69,000 acres of land, transforming Tanjore into the rice bowl of South India.

Apart from agriculture, he developed ports on both the east and west coasts of the southern peninsula, which were connected through overland as well as sea routes. A verse from the Sangam period text *Puranānūru* suggests that the mariners of the Chola kingdom were well versed in using monsoon winds for their trade voyages. King Karikala's attention to sea trade enabled his empire to amass great wealth, especially from commerce with the Roman Empire. This wealth was not only used to fund military expeditions but also to build great cities. Karikala is reputed to have adorned the capital city of Kanchipuram with gold.

> After the death of King Karikala, the Chola kingdom faced a lingering and bitter conflict between two rival princes—Nalankilli and Nedunkilli—for the throne.

Nalankilli and Nedunkilli

After the death of King Karikala, the Chola kingdom faced a lingering and bitter conflict between two rival princes—Nalankilli and Nedunkilli—for the throne. During this war, Nalankilli besieged the city of Uraiyur, the capital of the kingdom under Nedunkilli. In response, Nedunkilli locked himself inside the fort and left his subjects to suffer as the city ran out of essential supplies. Sangam literature records a desperate appeal made to the king, urging him to end the siege through decisive action:

> Children cry for want of milk, the women plait their hair without flowers, the mansions of the city resound with the cries of people wailing for want of water. It is not possible to hold out any more here, you master of fleet steeds! If you would be kind, open the gates (to the enemy) saying 'This is yours'; if you would be heroic, open the gates and lead your soldiers out to victory; to be neither the one nor the other, to close the strong gates of the fort and to shut yourself up in a corner behind the high walls, this, when one thinks of it, is shameful indeed![4]

Finally, on the battlefields of Kariyar, where the Chola army defeated the Pandya and Chera kings, Nalankilli, who

---

[4] Kale, M.R. (trans.), *The Mudrarakshasa of Vishakhadatta: A Drama Translated from the Original Sanskrit*, Motilal Banarsidass, 1960, p. 55.

was a brave warrior and an able ruler, emerged victorious in both external and internal conflicts.

Rules to Rule

- **Courage may win you a throne, but only economic foresight can help you keep it**
  After his father's death, Karikala faced exile at the hands of his rivals. Years later, he reclaimed his rightful place and survived a life-threatening conspiracy. Displaying unwavering courage, he overcame his enemies and restored his rule. However, what truly defined his reign was the immense prosperity he ushered in. Through agricultural reforms and maritime trade, Karikala ensured that the Chola kingdom flourished economically. The construction of the Kallanai dam, the development of trade routes and the embellishment of cities like Kanchipuram were all hallmarks of his economic foresight. Great leaders build enduring legacies not only through conquest, but also by creating systems that sustain prosperity long after their reign ends.

- **A leader cannot afford to be indecisive when his people are in distress**
  After Karikalan's death, Nedunkilli chose to hide behind fort walls instead of confronting his enemies. The siege of Uraiyur led to great civilian suffering, prompting even his own people to demand action.

A true leader must act in times of crisis—whether by fighting or conceding. Even today, hesitation during crises can erode public trust—leaders are remembered not for avoiding hard choices, but for making them when it matters most.

6

Samudragupta

The Story

This is the tale of ancient India's most accomplished king—a military virtuoso and a true statesman. Excelling in both warfare and administration, Samudragupta achieved victory in a hundred battles, displaying remarkable strategic acumen. Beyond his conquests, he surpassed even the most celebrated poets of his time, earning renown as an erudite ruler and a discerning patron of music and art.

Rules to Rule

- Merit supersedes birthright in carving the path to greatness
- The finest commanders know when not to fight
- An empire thrives not by one rule, but by wise exceptions

The Foundation of the Gupta Empire

The Gupta dynasty began as a modest kingdom in parts of modern-day Bihar and Bengal, founded by Sri Gupta. His son, Ghatotkacha, initially served as a vassal to the declining Kushan Empire. The real turning point came with Ghatotkacha's ambitious son, Chandragupta I, who transformed the family's fortunes and laid the groundwork for one of India's greatest empires.

Around 320 CE, Chandragupta married a princess from the influential Licchavi clan. The Licchavis—an ancient ruling family that once led the Vajji Mahajanapada from Vaishali—had declined in power but remained prestigious. This alliance brought political legitimacy, wealth and military backing, greatly strengthening the Gupta dynasty's position in northern India.

> Breaking with tradition, Chandragupta convened a council of advisors, who unanimously chose Samudragupta based on merit—not lineage.

At the time, the Indian subcontinent was fragmented. The Kushan and Satavahana empires had weakened, leaving behind a mosaic of independent states vying for supremacy. Amid this instability, Chandragupta seized the moment. With Licchavi support and his own military ambitions, he expanded the Gupta realm, adopting the title 'Maharajadhiraja'—signifying his dominance over rival kings. His conquests extended as far west as Allahabad, solidifying a foundation that would soon usher in a golden age.

The Genius King

Chandragupta died around 340 CE, leaving behind a firmly established kingdom. His successor, Samudragupta, was born to Chandragupta and Princess Kumaradevi. However, his ascension was anything but assured. His elder brother Kaccha had a legitimate claim to the throne. Breaking with tradition, Chandragupta convened a council of advisors, who unanimously chose Samudragupta based on merit—not lineage. This pivotal decision set the stage for the rise of a ruler whose leadership would shape Indian history.

Military Conquests

Once on the throne, Samudragupta launched an aggressive campaign to consolidate northern India. According to the Allahabad Pillar inscription, he defeated nine regional kings:

- Rudrasen
- Matil
- Chandravarman
- Achyuta
- Ganpati
- Nagadutta
- Nagsen

- Nandin
- Balvarman

While little is known about these rulers, their defeat marked Samudragupta's emergence as the dominant power in the Gangetic plains. His success prompted surrounding regions—such as Bengal, Assam, Nepal—and tribal republics—like the Malavas, Yaudheyas, Arjunayanas, Madras and Abhiras—to voluntarily submit to Gupta supremacy.

> Samudragupta's genius extended beyond warfare.

Southern Conquests: Strategy over Suppression

With northern India secure, Samudragupta shifted his focus southward—not with the aim of annexation, but as a calculated display of might. His campaigns stretched from Madhya Pradesh to the Pallava kingdom of Kanchi—covering modern Ganjam, Visakhapatnam and Nellore—nourished by the Godavari and Krishna rivers. These southern expeditions defeated numerous rulers but he reinstated them as vassals, showcasing his preference for dominance over destruction.

Mastering Governance

Samudragupta's genius extended beyond warfare. He adopted a flexible administrative model tailored to India's vast and varied landscape. Rather than enforcing strict central control, he divided the empire into four categories:

- **Directly Administered States**—Governed by the emperor and his council.
- **Tributary States**—Local rulers retained power in exchange for regular tributes.
- **Reinstated States**—The conquered kingdoms in the south which were allowed to retain their rulers under Gupta suzerainty.
- **Allied or Independent States**—Regions like the Saka and Kushan territories that recognized Gupta supremacy while maintaining autonomy.

This nuanced model of decentralized governance allowed local autonomy while reinforcing Gupta paramountcy. It helped maintain peace across a culturally and politically diverse subcontinent.

Diplomacy and Cultural Soft Power

Samudragupta's influence extended beyond borders. As his reputation grew, neighbouring rulers sought Gupta favour. Some gained the right to use the Garuda seal—symbol of imperial endorsement—while others, like King Meghvarna of Sri Lanka, sent diplomatic envoys bearing tribute. Meghvarna even requested permission to build rest houses and monasteries at Bodh Gaya for Sri Lankan pilgrims, which Samudragupta graciously approved. These gestures of magnanimity strengthened cultural ties and cemented his status as a benevolent hegemon.

The Seven Coins: Emblems of Empire

Samudragupta's coinage tells the story of a multidimensional ruler. He issued seven types of coins, each capturing an aspect of his identity:

- **Archer Type**—Depicting him with a bow and arrow, symbolizing military skill.
- **Battle Axe Type**—Featuring a battle axe and a dwarf, representing domination.
- **Tiger Slayer Type**—Depicting him defeating a tiger, showcasing raw courage.
- **Ashwamedha Type**—Commemorating the horse sacrifice ritual of imperial authority.
- **Standard Type**—Showing fire worship beside the Garuda standard of power.
- **Veena Player Type**—Depicting him playing the veena, reflecting his musical talent.
- **Kaviraj Type**—Celebrating his literary prowess as 'King of Poets'.

These coins weren't mere currency—they were declarations of a ruler who fused force with finesse.

Inscriptions and Legacy

Beyond coins, inscriptions like those at Eran and Allahabad celebrated Samudragupta's generosity, sense of justice and devotion to dharma. The Eran inscription compares his gifts to those of legendary kings, while the Allahabad Pillar praises his efforts to uplift the downtrodden. These tributes underscore a ruler who combined military brilliance with benevolence.

Samudragupta's reign blended conquest with compassion, control with culture. He was not just a king of battles, but a ruler of balance—his legacy helped shape the golden age of ancient India.

Rules to Rule

- **Merit supersedes birthright in carving the path to greatness**
  Samudragupta's selection over his elder brother changed the course of Indian history. Leadership chosen by merit, not inheritance, paved the way for an age of excellence. In any era, the most enduring leadership rests on ability and vision rather than entitlement.

- **The finest commanders know when not to fight**
  Samudragupta avoided costly battles with powerful states like the Kadambas and Western Gangas. Instead, he built alliances, proving that real strength lay in

restraint. The wisest leaders recognize that restraint, not aggression, often secures the most lasting victories.

- **An empire thrives not by one rule, but by wise exceptions**
From direct rule to diplomatic vassalage, Samudragupta tailored governance to each region. Flexibility—not rigidity—kept the empire strong and stable. Effective leadership requires adjusting methods to suit the moment, while staying true to a larger purpose.

7

Chandragupta II

The Story

This is the story of a courageous prince who ventured into the heart of the enemy's camp with a small band of loyal soldiers. His mission was to rescue his brother's wife and protect the honour of the Gupta dynasty.

> ### Rules to Rule
> - Honour outweighs position
> - Prolonged conflict weakens the state

The Queen Dhruvswamini

Dhruvswamini (also known as Dhruva Devi) was the wife of King Ramgupta, the eldest son and successor of

Samudragupta. Renowned for her charm and beauty, she became the object of a humiliating diplomatic exchange when a Saka king, having defeated Ramgupta in battle, demanded her in return for peace. To the shock and disgrace of the empire, Ramgupta agreed and handed over his queen.

Unwilling to become the consort of the Saka king, Dhruvswamini was taken by force to the enemy camp. The younger prince, Chandragupta II, could not tolerate this humiliation of the Gupta dynasty. Defying his brother's orders, he disguised himself, infiltrated the enemy camp, and personally killed the Saka king. Dhruvswamini was safely returned, but she refused to live with Ramgupta, having lost all respect for him.

With Chandragupta II's heroism celebrated, public support turned against Ramgupta. His loss of honour and legitimacy created deep rivalries between the brothers. Eventually, Ramgupta was killed and Chandragupta II married Dhruvswamini, assuming the Gupta throne under the title 'Vikramaditya'.

Restoration of Glory

Chandragupta II revived the greatness of the Gupta Empire, restoring the legacy of his father, Samudragupta. His military campaigns expanded the empire's boundaries and secured its trade routes.

In the west, he launched a major offensive against the Sakas, expelling them from India. He defeated and killed Rudrasimha III, annexing western Malwa and Kathiawad. His victories extended the empire to the Arabian Sea, incorporating vital ports such as Broach, Sopara and Cambay, facilitating trade with the Roman Empire.

In the north, his campaigns took him through Punjab, reaching as far as Balkh in modern Afghanistan. An inscription on the sacred rock of Hunza—'Chandra Shri Vikramaditya Conquers'—suggests his control over the trade route from Central Asia to India.

In the east, he secured Vanga (present-day Bengal), a region known for war elephants and maritime dominance over the Bay of Bengal.

In the south, rather than relying solely on warfare, he used strategic matrimonial alliances. He married his daughter, Prabhavatigupta, to the Vakataka king Rudrasena II, gaining influence in the Deccan. Similarly, he forged ties with the Kadamba dynasty by marrying his son, Kumaragupta, to Anantadevi, daughter of the Kadamba king Kakusthavarman.

The Great Reformer

Chandragupta II was not just a warrior—he was a visionary leader. His reforms in military, administration, trade and culture strengthened the Gupta Empire's golden age.

He modernized the Gupta army, drawing inspiration from Kushan military techniques. Troops were outfitted with turbans instead of helmets, Scythian-style trousers, high boots and camouflage gear for stealth.

> Chandragupta II's court became a centre of literary and cultural brilliance.

Administratively, he blended Mauryan and Scythian governance models. The empire was divided into provinces ruled by *uparika*s, districts headed by *vishayapati*s, and villages governed by a council led by a *gramika*. Land revenue, one-sixth of cultivation, formed the financial backbone of the empire.

Economically, he supported trade guilds, empowering *shreshti*s (bankers), *kulika*s (merchants) and *sarthavaha*s (caravan leaders). Metallurgy thrived during his reign, reaching new heights of sophistication.

The Iron Pillar of Delhi—a 7.16-metre, rust-free iron monument crafted from 99.7 per cent pure wrought iron—stands as a testament to Gupta metallurgy. Its inscription commemorates Chandragupta II's achievements.

The Great Court of Chandragupta II

Chandragupta II's court became a centre of literary and cultural brilliance. Kalidasa, the greatest Sanskrit poet and playwright, served as his court poet. Viresena, his chief minister, played a crucial role in foreign affairs and statecraft. The author of *Kamandakiya Niti*, a renowned political treatise, also flourished under his patronage.

While legends speak of a 'Navaratna' (nine-gem) council under his reign, historical evidence is inconclusive. Nevertheless, his court undeniably fostered intellectual and artistic excellence.

The Visit of Faxian

The Chinese Buddhist monk Faxian visited India during Chandragupta II's reign. His travelogue offers valuable insights into Gupta prosperity and governance.

According to Faxian, the people of Madhya-Desh lived in prosperity and harmony. Bureaucratic interference was minimal—only the cultivators of royal land were required to pay tribute. Corporal punishment was rare; fines were the common penalty. Only in cases of repeated rebellion was a right hand amputated.

He also recorded the presence of charitable institutions in cities, supported by wealthy Vaishya families. These offered food and medicine to the poor, diseased, orphaned and widowed—underscoring the empire's culture of compassion and social welfare.

The Declining Path

Kumaragupta, son of Dhruvswamini and successor to Chandragupta II, initially upheld the empire's stability.

He conducted the *Ashvamedha* sacrifice and sought to expand the empire's influence. He launched campaigns in Dasha Pura (modern Mandasur) and possibly conquered Kamarupa (modern Assam), as suggested by coins depicting him slaying a rhinoceros.

However, in the later years of his reign, the empire faced mounting threats. A confederacy called the 'Yudhyamitras' (possibly including the Vakatakas) challenged Gupta authority near the Narmada. Simultaneously, the northwestern frontier faced invasions from the Shweta Hunas (Hephthalites or Kidarites).

As Kumaragupta aged, his son Skandagupta assumed military command. He defeated the Yudhyamitras, as described in the Bhitari Pillar inscription. He also repelled the Hunas and assumed the title Vikramaditya, like his grandfather.

These victories came at a steep price. The empire's treasury was severely depleted, and trade with Central Asia and Europe suffered. By the time Skandagupta died in AD 467, the Hunas had become a major threat. His successor, Purugupta, failed to contain them. Their invasion led to the disintegration of the Gupta Empire and a period of instability across northern India.

Rules to Rule

- **Honour outweighs position**
  Power earned without integrity is fragile. Ramgupta's failure to defend his queen led to disgrace, while Chandragupta's brave defiance restored the dynasty's honour. Courage, not compromise, earns true loyalty and legitimacy. When faced with moral crisis, leadership is tested by action, not excuses.

- **Prolonged conflict weakens the state**
  Skandagupta won battles but lost stability. Endless wars drained resources, disrupted trade and diverted attention away from governance. Victory must be balanced with sustainability—when wars become a habit, decline often follows.

8

Prabhavatigupta

The Story

This is the story of Prabhavatigupta, the exceptionally resilient daughter of Chandragupta II, one of India's most illustrious emperors. She embodied her father's vision and strength, supporting not just his imperial ambitions but also those of her in-laws—all while enduring profound personal grief. Her life is a testament to quiet power, strategic foresight and maternal resilience in the face of recurring loss.

Rules to Rule

- In times of upheaval, steady hands must guide uncertain feet

Unwavering Commitment to Expelling the Sakas from India

The Sakas (Western Kshatrapas) were a persistent thorn in the side of the Gupta Empire. Years earlier, they had captured Queen Dhruvadevi, prompting Chandragupta II to rescue her in a daring campaign. Determined to eliminate this long-standing threat, Chandragupta launched an offensive that initially succeeded in driving the Sakas out of northern and central India—but they remained entrenched in the western regions.

At this time, Rudrasimha III, the Saka ruler, still held control over western Malwa and Kathiawad. To dislodge them completely, Chandragupta II pursued a strategic alliance with the Vakatakas—powerful successors of the Satavahanas who ruled an expansive empire stretching from northern Malwa and Gujarat to the Tungabhadra River in the Deccan.

To cement this alliance, Chandragupta II arranged the marriage of his daughter, Prabhavatigupta, to the Vakataka prince Rudrasena II. The Vakataka king, Prithvisena I, eagerly accepted the proposal from the most dominant power of the age.

A Dynasty United by Naga Lineage

Prabhavatigupta's mother, Kubernaga, belonged to the powerful Naga dynasty, known for their role in resisting the Kushans in North and Central India. This shared Naga ancestry further reinforced the Gupta-Vakataka alliance.

Prabhavatigupta soon proved herself to be a formidable political figure.

- When Samudragupta defeated the Nagas at Mathura, they submitted to Gupta rule. As part of the resulting peace, Princess Kubernaga married Chandragupta II.
- On the Vakataka side, Prabhavatigupta's grandfather-in-law, Rudrasena I, was the son of a Naga princess from Padmavati—daughter of King Bhava Naga of the Bharsiva clan.

These shared bloodlines may have influenced Chandragupta II's decision to ally with the Vakatakas—a move that became central to his campaign against the Sakas.

Assuming Charge of the Kingdom at 25

In 385 CE, five years after her marriage, Prithvisena I passed away, and Rudrasena II ascended the Vakataka throne with Prabhavatigupta as his chief queen. By then, she had given birth to three sons and wielded significant influence. At her request, Rudrasena II converted from Shaivism to Vaishnavism.

But Rudrasena II's reign was cut short—he died suddenly after only five years on the throne. Grieving yet composed, Prabhavatigupta received her father at the Vakataka capital. Chandragupta II's presence ensured her smooth transition into power as regent for her minor sons, Divakarsena and Damodarsena.

Though only 25 years old, and lacking formal administrative experience, she quickly adapted. Officers from Pataliputra likely assisted her in court affairs. The famed poet Kalidasa was even sent to educate her sons, a mark of how seriously Chandragupta II took the future of this alliance.

> As the daughter of a king and the matriarch of an empire, Prabhavatigupta held power not by force, but by trust, wisdom and sacrifice.

Prabhavatigupta soon proved herself to be a formidable political figure. Working in tandem with her father, she helped block Saka movement through Vakataka territory, enabling Chandragupta II to sweep through Gujarat and Kathiawad, bringing an end to three centuries of Saka rule in India.

The Resilient Queen

Shortly after this triumph, tragedy struck again: her eldest son, Divakarsena, died suddenly. Once more, Prabhavatigupta was left to steady the empire and continue her regency until her second son, Damodarsena, came of age. She governed effectively for more than two decades, maintaining peace and continuity until 410 CE, when

Damodarsena formally took the throne.

But fate remained cruel—Damodarsena died barely 10 years into his reign. Prabhavatigupta intervened again, ensuring her third son, Pravarasena II, succeeded the throne. Her enduring leadership anchored the dynasty through multiple crises, earning her the admiration of both allies and adversaries.

During Pravarasena II's reign, the Kadambas emerged as a formidable force in North Kannada and the Konkan. The Vakatakas and Kadambas had long contested the fertile Krishna-Tungabhadra delta. Understanding the need for lasting peace, Prabhavatigupta arranged the marriage of her grandson, Narendrasena, to the Kadamba princess Ajitabhattarika—a strategic move that ended hostilities and ensured regional stability.

As the daughter of a king and the matriarch of an empire, Prabhavatigupta held power not by force, but by trust, wisdom and sacrifice. She lived for nearly a century, safeguarding her kingdom through war, succession and sorrow.

In her later years, she retired from politics and devoted herself to religion, particularly in worship of the deity Ramagirisvamin, associated with Ramtek near Nagpur.

Thus was the remarkable life of one of the most courageous and steadfast queens in Indian history.

Rules to Rule

- **In times of upheaval, steady hands must guide uncertain feet**

   When leadership transitions are marred by grief or uncertainty, rival forces often sense an opportunity to strike. After Rudrasena II's death, it was Prabhavatigupta's resilience—backed by her father's vision and the quiet guidance of experienced hands—that preserved the Vakataka realm. She ruled not as a placeholder, but as a leader who brought both continuity and reform.

   Change invites instability in modern institutions as well. But when a steady presence takes the reins—one that combines legacy with foresight—it creates the space for new leadership to mature without disruption. The hand that holds, also shapes.

9

Kanishka

The Story

This is the story of a glorious Buddhist king whose dynasty—once nomadic tribes from the Qilian Mountains of China—came to rule vast swathes of northern India for over three centuries. Under Kanishka, the Kushan Empire expanded from southern Uzbekistan to the Gangetic plains, with its influence touching warfare, governance, art and spiritual life. His reign shaped the course of history not only through conquest but also through cultural exchange and religious patronage.

Rules to Rule

- The flapping of a butterfly's wings can cause a tornado

- The interests of politics and religion are often different
- Four universal factors are responsible for the decline of an empire

The Great Migration of Yuezhi and Sakas

In the rugged region between the Qilian Mountains and the city of Dunhuang—in modern-day Gansu, China—nomadic tribes like the Yuezhi, Wusun and Xiongnu competed for grazing lands. In 174 BCE, the powerful Xiongnu defeated the Yuezhi, forcing them to migrate southwest—a shift that would eventually reshape the politics of Central and South Asia.

As they moved, the Yuezhi clashed with the Sakas near the Ili River. Pushed out, the Sakas migrated into Bactria. But the Yuezhi's hold there was brief. In 132 BCE, the Wusun—allied with the Xiongnu—attacked again, driving the Yuezhi further into the Oxus River region (modern-day Amu Darya).

Meanwhile, in 145 BCE, the Sakas crossed the Jaxartes River and attacked the Greco-Bactrian kingdom. Their invasion devastated Alexandria and marked the beginning of Greco-Bactrian decline. Soon after, the Yuezhi were pushed south into Bactria, displacing the Sakas once again. The Sakas dispersed—some toward Parthia and others into the Hindu Kush, where they conquered the last Indo-Greek kingdoms.

Establishment of the Kushan Dynasty

For generations, the Yuezhi ruled as a confederation of five sub-tribes, expanding and fragmenting in equal measure. But in 30 CE, Prince Kujula Kadphises of the Kushan tribe unified them, founding the kingdom of the Kushans.

> Kanishka inherited not only a powerful army but a vast and thriving realm.

Intent on expansion, the Kushans advanced into Parthian territory, seizing the valley of Kabul—a vital gateway to India. Upon Kujula's death, his son Vima Takto led an army of 100,000 mounted archers across the Indus. Their swift, agile forces outmanoeuvred Indian war elephants, securing sweeping victories across the north.

By 100 CE, Vima Kadphises had ascended the throne, extending the empire further between the Indus and Ganges. In 127 CE, his successor Kanishka inherited not only a powerful army but a vast and thriving realm. Coins and inscriptions bearing his name—found across Mathura, Patna and Gaya—attest to his authority over northern India.

Expansion under Kanishka

Kanishka's campaigns were as strategic as they were expansive,

> Kanishka's reign saw the highest volume of gold coins of the era—Roman in style, depicting deities from India, Persia and Rome—a reflection of rich cultural and commercial fusion.

aimed at controlling vital trade routes that linked Central Asia, India, the Middle East and Europe.

- **Securing the Uttarapath (Northern High Road):** He brought the whole expanse between Bactria and Pataliputra under Kushan control, including the cities of Mathura, Shravasti, Kaushambi, Varanasi and Vaishali.
- **Dominating the Tarim Basin:** A critical Silk Road hub, this gave the Kushans leverage over trade from China to India.
- **Controlling Bharuch Port:** Situated on the Narmada River, this port facilitated maritime trade with Rome.
- **Founding New Cities:** He established Sirmukh (near Taxila), Puruspur (modern Peshawar) and Kanishkpur (in Kashmir).

Through these conquests, Kanishka commanded one of the greatest trade networks in history. His reign saw the highest volume of gold coins of the era—Roman in style, depicting deities from India, Persia and Rome—a reflection of rich cultural and commercial fusion.

Patronage of Buddhism

Kanishka's turn toward Buddhism recalls the transformation of Mauryan Emperor Ashoka. After defeating the Parthian king Vologases III, Kanishka was shaken by the bloodshed and sought spiritual guidance. He turned to the monk Ashvaghosa and became one of the greatest Buddhist patrons in Indian history.

- He convened the Fourth Buddhist Council at Kundalgram in Kashmir, presided over by Vasumitra.
- He commissioned a monumental stupa near Peshawar which was built with the help of Greek artisans.
- He supported Buddhist merchants, enabling the spread of Buddhism across the Silk Road, from India into China.

Unlike Ashoka, however, Kanishka did not renounce warfare. Even after embracing Buddhism, he led a military expedition against the Han dynasty, attempting to conquer Kashgar. He was ultimately defeated by the Chinese general Ban Chao and forced to pay tribute to Emperor Ho-Ti.

Decline of the Empire

After Kanishka's death, his son Huvishka ruled in peace, strengthening Kushan influence in Mathura. But his successor, Vasudeva I, struggled to maintain unity within the Yuezhi confederation. Under his reign:

- The western provinces fell to the Indo-Sassanids (Kushanshahs).

- Control of Silk Road trade routes diminished, leading to economic decline.
- Local powers like the Arjunayanas and Yaudheyas reasserted independence.
- In 335 CE, Samudragupta defeated the last Kushan king, marking the end of the dynasty.

Rules to Rule

- **The flapping of a butterfly's wings can cause a tornado**
  Small shifts in one part of the world can reshape empires. The Yuezhi migration—triggered by tribal warfare in Central Asia—displaced the Sakas, collapsed the Greco-Bactrian kingdom, and birthed the Kushan Empire. These cascading movements redefined the politics of South and Central Asia for centuries. In modern systems—be it business, governance, or diplomacy—seemingly distant disruptions can trigger unexpected upheaval. A wise leader monitors the margins, not just the centre.

- **The interests of politics and religion are often different**
  Kanishka balanced both. While Ashoka renounced war for spiritual pursuits, Kanishka expanded his empire even after adopting Buddhism. His ability to separate personal faith from political strategy preserved imperial strength while spreading spiritual influence.

Leaders today often walk a similar tightrope: balancing personal conviction with institutional responsibility. The lesson is not withdrawal, but discernment.

- **Four universal factors are responsible for the decline of an empire**

    The Kushan Empire, despite its glory, collapsed under the weight of four universal forces: an incapable successor, external invasions, economic decline and over-expansion. Vasudeva I's weak leadership fractured the Yuezhi confederation. The Indo-Sassanids eroded military strength. The loss of the Silk Road trade routes crippled the economy. And a vast, unwieldy empire proved impossible to sustain. In every field, growth without consolidation breeds collapse. The empires that last are the ones that pace their ambition with reflection.

10

Gautamiputra Satakarni

The Story

This is the story of a legendary king, remembered in history primarily through his mother's name, Queen Gautami of the Satavahana dynasty. However, this was not because he was a mere figurehead while his mother ruled. Rather, it was her immense pride in his bravery, leadership and achievements that forever linked their names in history.

> ### Rules to Rule
>
> - Conquering a powerful adversary requires support from all possible directions
> - To restore past glory, it is essential to rectify present faults

- Alliances do not guarantee peace—self-interest always takes precedence

The Satavahanas

The Satavahanas, also referred to as the Andhras in the Puranas, ruled over Dakshinapatha (the Deccan region) for over three centuries, from the first century BCE to the third century CE. Following the decline of the Mauryan Empire, Simuka founded the Satavahana dynasty in the upper Godavari region, with Pratishthan (modern-day Paithan) as its capital.

> Naganika holds the distinction of being the first queen in world history to mint coins bearing her name.

Simuka was succeeded by his brother Kanha, as his own son was too young to rule at the time. Kanha proved to be a capable ruler and expanded the empire significantly. His reign lasted for 18 years, during which Satakarni I, the son of Simuka, came of age and was formally installed as king.

Satakarni I ruled for only six years. After his death, his wife Naganika assumed control of the kingdom on behalf of their son, Satakarni II. Notably, she commissioned the Sanskrit inscriptions at Naneghat in the Brahmi script. Naneghat, a mountain pass in the Western Ghats between the Konkan coast and Junnar on the Deccan plateau, houses these inscriptions. Naganika holds the distinction of being the first queen in world history to mint coins bearing her name.

When Satakarni II came of age, he assumed power and ruled for around 50 years. He was a capable ruler who successfully defended his territory against the campaigns of Kalinga king Kharavela. After Kharavela's death, he expanded his dominion into Avanti and Kalinga. To the north of the Narmada River, he conquered eastern Malwa after defeating the kingdom of the Sungas and extended his rule to Sanchi, where he added decorated gateways to the stupa built by Emperor Ashoka. In the south, he conquered the Godavari Valley and assumed the title of 'Dakshinapati' (lord of the southern region).

> Gautamiputra Satakarni, son of King Sivasvati and Queen Gautami Balashri, was born during a time of unrest following a century of peace.

However, his successors lacked his military prowess. Between Satakarni II and Gautamiputra Satakarni, only King Hala stands out for compiling an anthology of Maharashtri Prakrit poems known as the *Gatha Saptasati*. The Satavahana rulers during this period struggled against foreign invaders, particularly the Greeks, Sakas and Parthians. Toward the end of the first century CE, the Saka chiefs, known as the Western Kshatraps, expelled the Satavahanas from Malwa and captured northwestern Deccan, including Nasik.

At this critical juncture, Gautamiputra Satakarni ascended the Satavahana throne.

Restoration of Satavahana Glory

Gautamiputra Satakarni, son of King Sivasvati and Queen Gautami Balashri, was born during a time of unrest following a century of peace. Sivasvati, who ruled for around 28 years, had suffered defeat at the hands of the Western Kshatrapas and lost Pune and Nasik. After his father's death, Gautamiputra ascended the throne and immediately set out to revive Satavahana power.

He enlarged the army, transforming it into a formidable, battle-hardened force. Demonstrating personal courage, he boosted morale and led successful campaigns against the Saka ruler Nahapana. Under his leadership, Nahapana was defeated and forced to withdraw from Maharashtra. Territories seized by the Sakas were recovered, and Nahapana's coins were overstruck with Gautamiputra's name. The Nasik inscription describes him as the king who vanquished the Sakas, Yavanas and Pallavas. It also records that his dominion stretched from Malwa and Saurashtra in the north to the Krishna River in the south, and from Berar in the east to the Konkan coast in the west. He adopted the titles 'Raja-Raja' (king of kings) and 'Maharaja' (great king), and was called the sovereign of the Vindhyas.

> Gautamiputra addressed administrative weaknesses by decentralizing the Mauryan-style centralized governance.

Gautamiputra addressed administrative weaknesses by

decentralizing the Mauryan-style centralized governance. He created smaller administrative units called *ahara*s and empowered officials like *amatya*s, *mahamatra*s, *mahasenapati* and *maha-talvara*s. This structure enabled more effective governance, especially during times of external threats.

Religiously, Gautamiputra supported both Vedic traditions and the Buddhist sangha. The Nasik inscription refers to him as 'Ekbamhana', denoting his affinity with Brahmanical practices. At the same time, he donated land and resources to Buddhist monks and built caves along trade routes for both traders and monks. His inclusive approach bolstered political stability.

Economically, he reduced taxes to strengthen bonds with his people and encouraged trade to offset revenue losses. He sought control over strategic ports like Bhrigukaccha (Broach), Kalyan and Suparaka (Sopara), expanding trade with regions like Malay, Shyam, Sumatra, Bali and even the Roman Empire. New trading cities emerged, and river ports along the Vamsadhara, Godavari and Krishna rivers improved inland-to-port logistics. Trade flourished in hubs such as Pratishthan, Nasik, Tagar and Karhatak.

> The Junagadh inscription of Rudradaman I states that he defeated Satakarni, the 'lord of Dakshinapatha', twice.

Sustained Struggle with the Sakas

The struggle with the Sakas continued after Gautamiputra's death. His son, Vasishthiputra Pulumavi, failed to retain Avanti and Ujjain, which were seized by the Saka ruler Castana, who had allied with Kushan emperor Kanishka. Pulumavi's successor, Vashishtiputra Satakarni, also suffered defeat at the hands of Rudradaman I, Castana's grandson. The Junagadh inscription of Rudradaman I states that he defeated Satakarni, the 'lord of Dakshinapatha', twice.

Despite a matrimonial alliance—Vashishtiputra Satakarni married Rudradaman's daughter—conflict persisted. The Junagadh inscription notes that Rudradaman spared the defeated Satavahana king due to their familial bond. Gautamiputra's grandson, Yajna Satakarni, later revived Satavahana fortunes by defeating Rudrasimha I, reclaiming much of the lost territory, including parts of the Konkan, Deccan and Central Provinces.

However, after Yajna Satakarni's death, the empire fractured into smaller dominions ruled by Satavahana family branches. These were eventually supplanted by emerging powers such as the Abhiras in northwest Deccan, the Ikshvakus between the Krishna and Godavari rivers, the Brihhatpahalayans in Muslipatnam, the Pallavas near Kanchi, and the Vakatakas in the broader Deccan region.

Rules to Rule

- **Conquering a powerful adversary requires support from all possible directions**

  Gautamiputra's success in defeating the formidable Saka ruler Nahapana was not due to military strength alone. He strategically built alliances with local powers like the Kuras, Anandas and Hastis—minor but influential dynasties and aristocrats like the Maharathis and Mahabhojas. These alliances gave him access to resources, troops and local support. The broader lesson here is that confronting powerful adversaries often requires collective strength and support from multiple directions. No leader, however strong, wins alone.

- **To restore past glory, it is essential to rectify present faults**

  To restore the crumbling glory of the Satavahana Empire, Gautamiputra had to first address its internal weaknesses. He recognized that the over-centralized Mauryan-style governance no longer suited the times. By decentralizing administration, reducing tax burdens and empowering regional officials, he stabilized his realm and gained the confidence of his people. History teaches us that sustainable revival often depends on first acknowledging and correcting present faults, rather than merely invoking the greatness of the past.

- **Alliances do not guarantee peace—self-interest always takes precedence**
  Even though Vashishtiputra Satakarni married the daughter of Rudradaman I, this matrimonial alliance failed to bring lasting peace. The Junagadh inscription records that Rudradaman defeated the Satavahana king twice, though he spared his life due to familial ties. But hostilities resumed, and it was only in the next generation that Gautamiputra's grandson, Yajna Satakarni, reclaimed lost territory. This shows us that alliances built for diplomacy or convenience often crumble in the face of self-interest. True peace and cooperation come not from alliances alone but from aligned objectives and mutual respect.

11

Harshavardhana

The Story

Harshavardhana was one of the greatest kings of North India, a man of literary pursuits who never initially contemplated engaging in matters of war and politics. However, circumstances forced him to assume the throne and restore the declining affairs of the empire he inherited.

Rules to Rule

- Special circumstances require special responses; business as usual cannot continue
- Misjudgement of challenges inevitably paves the way for defeat
- True greatness lies in recognizing and respecting others

The Rise of the Pushyabhutis

After the decline of the Gupta Empire, four major powers emerged in North India: the Guptas of Magadha (distinct from the original Gupta dynasty), the Mukharis of Kannauj, the Maitrakas of Valabhi and the Pushyabhutis of Thaneshwar. The Pushyabhutis, however, reached their pinnacle under the reign of Harshavardhana.

> Harsha was the great-grandson of King Adityavardhan, ruler of the ancient city of Kurukshetra...

Harsha was the great-grandson of King Adityavardhan, ruler of the ancient city of Kurukshetra, also known as Sthaneshwar or Thaneshwar. Adityavardhan, the third ruler of the Pushyabhuti dynasty, strengthened his family's position through a strategic marriage to Princess Mahasena Gupta of Magadha. This alliance significantly enhanced the power and prestige of the Pushyabhuti family.

His son, Prabhakaravardhana, leveraged this influence to expand his territories, extending his rule over the entire Punjab region in the northwest and a portion of Malwa in the south. He was a wise ruler who understood the importance of alliances in consolidating his kingdom's strength. Prabhakaravardhana further solidified his position by marrying his daughter, Rajyashri, to Grahavarman, the Mukhari king.

Additionally, Prabhakaravardhana maintained close ties with King Mahasengupta of Magadha.

> Shashanka of the Gauda dynasty emerged as a formidable power in Bengal, aggressively expanding into North India...

When Mahasengupta was displaced—possibly due to a coup—Prabhakaravardhana granted refuge to his two sons, Kumargupta and Mahadevgupta. These young princes developed strong bonds of friendship with Prabhakaravardhana's sons, Rajyavardhana and Harshavardhana. This alliance would later prove crucial in the Pushyabhutis' future endeavours.

Intense Clashes with King Shashanka of Bengal

After Prabhakaravardhana's death, his elder son, Rajyavardhana, ascended the throne. Around the same time, Shashanka of the Gauda dynasty emerged as a formidable power in Bengal, aggressively expanding into North India, threatening the interests of the Mukharis and Pushyabhutis.

Shashanka swiftly attacked and captured Kannauj, defeating the Mukhari army and killing King Grahavarman. Queen Rajyashri was taken prisoner. Enraged, Rajyavardhana immediately led a cavalry force of 10,000 soldiers to reclaim Kannauj. On the way, he defeated Devgupta, the King of Malwa, who had allied with Shashanka. However, as Rajyavardhana advanced with a smaller force, he was ambushed and killed by Shashanka.

The news of Rajyavardhana's death shook the

Pushyabhuti capital city of Sthaneshwar (Thaneshwar). Prabhakaravardhana's younger son, Harshavardhana, initially had no desire to assume the throne. He was a man of literary interests and had never contemplated involvement in the affairs of war and politics. However, faced with such a dire situation, he had no choice but to summon the courage and valour necessary to rescue his sister and restore the crumbling empire. He assumed the position of king and made a solemn oath before his court that if he failed to eliminate the Gauda clan of Shashanka, he would set himself on fire.

With such a harsh decision, Harsha made every possible effort to fulfil his pledge. He organized a formidable army, reportedly consisting of 60,000 elephants and 100,000 cavalry, as recorded by the accounts of Hiuen Tsang. Additionally, he reached out to Bhaskaravarman, the king of Kamarupa, requesting his assistance in the campaign against the king of Bengal.

Bhaskaravarman, who himself felt threatened by the expanding power of Shashanka, accepted the alliance with Harsha.

During this time, Harsha received information that his sister, Rajyashri, had been released from prison. However, instead of returning to Sthaneshwar, she went to the Vindhya forest in anguish and despair. In response, Harsha immediately dispatched a mission to search for and rescue her. Just as she was about to throw herself into the fire, Rajyashri was spotted by Harsha's men and persuaded to return to Sthaneshwar.

Following this, Harsha launched a campaign eastward to avenge his brother's death. Shashanka, however, was a skilled military commander. Rather than engaging Harsha in direct combat, he tactically withdrew from Kannauj. With no Mukhari heir to reclaim the throne, the kingdom offered its crown to Harsha. He thus ruled over both the Pushyabhuti and Mukhari territories, relocating his capital from Sthaneshwar to Kannauj.

The Conflict over the Lata Region and the Battle of Narmada

Harsha, having solidified his rule in the north, set his sights on the west coast of India, particularly Bharuch in Gujarat, a strategic port city. He successfully occupied Vallabhi but chose to maintain peace with its ruling Maitraka dynasty through a matrimonial alliance, marrying one of his daughters to King Dhruvasena II Baladitya.

However, this alliance unsettled the Gurjars of the Lata region, who ruled Bharuch. Seeking protection, they sent tribute to Pulakeshin II of the Chalukya dynasty in the Deccan. Pulakeshin II, however, used this opportunity to gain control over the Lata region and its ports.

Harsha, seeing this as a threat to his trade ambitions, led an army to the banks of the Narmada River. Pulakeshin II, recognizing the difficulty of direct confrontation, used the river as a natural defence. The Aihole inscription describes how Pulakeshin II strategically positioned his forces to ambush Harsha at the crossing, leveraging the terrain to his advantage. Harsha struggled to make progress and, realizing the futility of prolonged conflict in the Deccan, agreed to a treaty. The Narmada River was established as the boundary between the Pushyabhuti and Chalukya empires.

> Harsha successfully extended his dominion from eastern Punjab to Odisha, encompassing present-day Uttar Pradesh, Bihar and much of West Bengal.

Harsha's Eastern Conquests

After his setback in the south, Harsha refocused on the east. Collaborating once again with Bhaskaravarman, he launched another campaign against Bengal following Shashanka's death. With no strong adversary left, Harsha successfully extended his dominion from eastern Punjab to Odisha, encompassing present-day Uttar Pradesh, Bihar and much of West Bengal.

Unlike Shashanka, who engaged in acts of religious aggression, such as cutting down the Bodhi Tree at Gaya, Harsha was known for his religious tolerance.

Though a follower of Shaivism, he patronized all religions and sects.

Saga of Greatness

> Harsha authored Sanskrit plays such as *Nagananda*, *Ratnavali* and *Priyadarshika*, which are still celebrated as masterpieces of classical Sanskrit literature.

It is a rare occurrence in history when a king is also a renowned writer, and Harsha embodied this distinction. He authored Sanskrit plays such as *Nagananda*, *Ratnavali* and *Priyadarshika*, which are still celebrated as masterpieces of classical Sanskrit literature. Simultaneously, in the tradition of great kings, he gathered a distinguished assembly of scholars in his court, including Banbhatta, Maui, Divakara and Jaysena. Banbhatta's works, *Kadambari* and *Harshacharita*, are regarded as some of the greatest pieces of Sanskrit literature. Harsha also played a key role in reviving support for Nalanda Mahavihara, which had declined since the Gupta Empire, generously granting several villages to ensure the institution's students and monks had the necessary provisions.

This learned king, in addition to his remarkable literary interests and astute military acumen, was also a vigilant administrator. He recognized that the security of trade and pilgrimage routes had significantly declined after the fall of the great Gupta Empire. Consequently, he made it a practice to embark on regular journeys throughout his empire to personally oversee state affairs and ensure the resolute handling of marauders and raiders. During one of these tours, he encountered the Chinese pilgrim Hiuen Tsang.

> Harsha made generous donations to Brahmins, Buddhist monks, the poor, orphans and destitute individuals. He even gave away his personal jewellery, including necklaces, earrings, bracelets, and more.

Meeting with Hiuen Tsang

During one of his tours to oversee state affairs on the ground, King Harsha encountered the Chinese pilgrim Hiuen Tsang. Hiuen Tsang was a Chinese scholar and traveller, and a devoted follower of Buddhist teachings. He was inspired by his compatriot Faxian, the renowned traveller who had brought original Buddhist texts to China. Hiuen Tsang aimed to continue the work of his predecessor to resolve discrepancies in Buddhist texts translated into Chinese. His journey began in 629 CE, and he crossed Central Asia to enter India via Kabul. Over his 16 years in India, he traversed the entire country, visiting nearly all the places associated with Buddhism.

Harsha, a great patron of knowledge, wisdom and learning, was delighted after meeting Hiuen Tsang. He extended an invitation to the traveller to participate in a special assembly at Kannauj. This grand conference lasted for a month and was organized in honour of the Chinese scholar. It provided a platform to discuss various ideas related to virtue, religion and life. A massive monastery was constructed to accommodate the numerous participants, including thousands of Buddhist monks, Jains and devout Brahmins. Atop a 100-foot tower, a golden image of Buddha was installed. Additionally, a temporary palace was constructed to host Emperor Harsha and 20 tributary kings.

The extravagant arrangements for this event sparked envy among a faction of Brahmins who believed that King Harsha was showing excessive favouritism towards Buddhism. Before the conclusion of the event, a group of extremists conspired to set the monastery on fire. While the king was inspecting the scene from the top of a stupa, he was attacked by one of these fanatics. Fortunately, the attempt to assassinate him failed, and the culprits were subsequently apprehended and punished.

Harsha concluded the conference after this unfortunate incident and then proceeded to Prayagraj along with Hiuen Tsang to participate in the grand pilgrimage festival known as the Kumbh, celebrated at the confluence of the Ganga and Yamuna rivers every five years. Here, as described by the Chinese pilgrim, King Harsha made generous donations to Brahmins, Buddhist monks, the poor, orphans and destitute individuals. He even gave away his personal jewellery, including necklaces, earrings, bracelets, and more. In the end, he requested an ordinary garment from his sister and donated even his own clothes to someone in need.

Rules to Rule

- **Special circumstances need special responses; business as usual cannot continue**
  When Harsha's brother and brother-in-law were killed, and his sister was abducted, he abandoned his literary life to take up arms and restore the honour of his family. His unyielding resolve in the face of crisis turned the tide of history, showing how extraordinary situations call for bold and decisive leadership.

- **Misjudging the scale of a challenge can lead to defeat**
  Despite his many victories, Harsha's campaign against Pulakeshin II failed because he underestimated the strategic challenge posed by the Narmada River. This setback reminds us that even strong leaders falter when they do not fully assess their adversaries or the terrain.

- **True greatness lies in recognizing and respecting others**
  Harsha honoured the wisdom and scholarship of Hiuen Tsang, extending hospitality and support that enhanced both their legacies. In contrast, his successor Arunasva disrespected a foreign envoy, leading to disastrous consequences. Leaders who treat others with respect build lasting alliances and legacies.

12

Pulakeshin II

The Story

It is the story of a prince who, at a young age, was banished by his own uncle after his father's demise. Not only did he effectively assert his rightful claim, but he also strengthened his position to the point where he proclaimed himself as the lord of Dakshinapatha.

> ### Rules to Rule
>
> - In intense conflicts, Kautilya's four-point strategy in warfare—*sama, dama, danda* and *bheda*—can prove decisive.
> - Elephants are not required to defeat elephants; cavalry can do so

The Regent Who Broke His Promise

Mangalesha was the brother of King Kirtivarman I, who ruled the Chalukya dynasty of Vatapi from 566 CE to 592 CE. When Kirtivarman passed away, his son Pulakeshin was still very young. To ensure a stable regency until the crown prince came of age, Mangalesha was appointed as regent.

Pulakeshin's mother, who was the sister of the Sendraka king, Shrivallabha Senanada, took her three sons to her brother's kingdom. Meanwhile, Mangalesha pursued an expansionist policy. He defeated the Kalachuris of Mahishmati, a region comprising parts of present-day Gujarat, Maharashtra and Madhya Pradesh. He further expanded northward, capturing southern Gujarat and the Nasik region. He also constructed a bridge of boats to cross the sea and conquer Revati Island in Maharashtra.

As often happens when one enjoys power for too long, Mangalesha forgot his pledge to relinquish the throne. When Pulakeshin asserted his claim, Mangalesha refused to step down. To further secure his hold, he placed his own son on the Chalukya throne and actively worked to keep Pulakeshin away from Vatapi. However, Pulakeshin, determined to reclaim his rightful place, gathered allies and launched a civil war. This culminated in Mangalesha's defeat and death, allowing Pulakeshin to ascend the throne.

Consolidation of Internal Power

> Pulakeshin's Chalukya navy, known for its formidable presence along the western coast, decisively defeated the invaders, thus ensuring that the Arab forces could not establish a foothold in the subcontinent.

Displacing Mangalesha did not mark the end of conflicts for Pulakeshin. Recognizing internal instability, rival factions sought to seize Chalukya territories. The Aihole inscription, written by the Jain poet Ravikirti, describes how 'the entire world was shrouded in the darkness of adversaries'. Yet, Pulakeshin's determination and strategic acumen allowed him to triumph over his enemies.

Pulakeshin employed Kautilya's *bheda* (divide and rule) strategy. Among the rebel leaders Appayika and Govinda, he convinced Govinda to switch sides, leading to Appayika's defeat. He also besieged Banavasi, the capital of the Kadamba dynasty, where King Bhogivarman resisted fiercely before finally being subdued after a prolonged blockade.

Pulakeshin did not stop at internal consolidation. One of his greatest achievements was repelling the first Arab invasion of India. The second caliph, Umar ibn Al-Khattab, intended to expand the Islamic Empire's influence, and his deputy, Usman, dispatched a naval expedition to Thane in Maharashtra. However, Pulakeshin's Chalukya navy, known for its formidable presence along the western coast, decisively defeated the invaders, thus ensuring that the Arab forces could not establish a foothold in the subcontinent.

Victory over Harshavardhana at the Battle of Narmada

As mentioned in the previous chapter, the Pushyabhuti king Harshavardhana, after conquering the city of Vallabhi, secured a matrimonial alliance with the Maitrakas. His ultimate objective was to expand his control over the Lata region, particularly the strategically significant port city of Bharuch.

However, the rulers of Lata were keenly aware of Harshavardhana's expansionist ambitions. Recognizing the rising power of Pulakeshin II, they sought his protection against Harsha's advances. Historically, the Lata region had previously been under the Kalachuris, who had already been defeated by Pulakeshin's predecessor, Mangalesha. Consequently, Pulakeshin II had legitimate claims over Lata, a region now contested by both the Chalukyas and the Pushyabhutis.

The Battle of Narmada

The forces of the Chalukyas and Pushyabhutis ultimately clashed at the Battle of Narmada. The southern region beyond the Narmada River was covered by the dense

Rather than engaging in a head-on clash of elephant contingents, Pulakeshin employed a tactical ambush, sending his infantry to disrupt and overpower Harsha's forces. This masterful strategy secured a decisive victory, forcing Harshavardhana to retreat in defeat.

forests of the Vindhyas, with rugged and difficult terrain that made large-scale battles challenging.

The Aihole inscription offers valuable insights into Pulakeshin II's military strategy during this battle. It poetically describes his elephants as so massive that they rivalled the Vindhya mountains themselves, suggesting that even nature seemed to bow before his power. The inscription also notes that Harshavardhana, usually confident, was gripped by fear as his elephants collapsed in battle.

Famed historian Nilakanta Sastri interprets these inscriptions as evidence that Pulakeshin II deliberately avoided deploying his elephants in the difficult Vindhya terrain. Instead, he stationed infantry to guard the mountain passes, utilizing the natural obstacles to his advantage. Rather than engaging in a head-on clash of elephant contingents, Pulakeshin employed a tactical ambush, sending his infantry to disrupt and overpower Harsha's forces. This masterful strategy secured a decisive victory, forcing Harshavardhana to retreat in defeat.

Chalukya Expansion in Central and Eastern India

Pulakeshin II's triumph at the Battle of Narmada significantly enhanced the Chalukya empire's authority, extending its dominance north of the Narmada River. The Aihole inscription records that the kings of Koshala and Kalinga accepted Pulakeshin II's suzerainty following this victory.

However, not all rulers submitted easily. The Vishnukundina kingdom, located in the lower Godavari-Krishna basin, resisted Pulakeshin's overlordship, leading to a fierce battle near Kolleru Lake. The Aihole inscription vividly describes how the waters of the lake turned red with the blood of fallen soldiers, a testament to the brutality of the conflict.

Following the defeat of the Vishnukundinas, Pulakeshin II appointed his younger brother, Vishnuvardhan, as the regent of the newly conquered territory, further consolidating Chalukya rule in southern India.

Conflict with the Pallavas and the fall of Pulakeshin II

The Chalukyas' military supremacy faced a significant challenge from the Pallavas, who defeated them on multiple occasions. However, it was Pulakeshin II who initiated the conflict by invading Pallava territories situated south of the

Chalukya domain. To strengthen his campaign, he forged alliances with the Chola, Chera and Pandya kings before leading his forces toward Kanchipuram, the Pallava capital.

The two armies clashed at Pallalura (modern Pullalur), but the battle ended without a decisive outcome. Although the Pallava king, Mahendravarman I, was forced to retreat toward Kanchipuram, his forces inflicted heavy damage on the Chalukyas. As a result, Pulakeshin II withdrew to Vatapi, marking the beginning of a prolonged and bitter rivalry.

Over time, deep-seated hostilities developed between the two kingdoms, leading to a series of fierce battles. This conflict extended beyond Pulakeshin II and Mahendravarman I, continuing through their descendants, ensuring that the rivalry between the Chalukyas and Pallavas persisted for generations.

After Mahendravarman I, his son Narasimhavarman I ascended the Pallava throne. In his thirteenth year of rule, he launched a well-planned offensive against the Chalukyas. Taking advantage of Pulakeshin II's absence from Vatapi, he dispatched his general, Shiruttondal Paranjoti, to besiege the Chalukya capital.

Paranjoti's forces successfully blockaded Vatapi, preparing for a prolonged confrontation. Upon hearing of the invasion, Pulakeshin II rushed back to defend his capital, but he failed to break through the Pallava army's formation. Ultimately, Paranjoti's forces overpowered Pulakeshin II, leading to his death and the fall of Vatapi to the Pallavas.

This marked the end of one of South India's most illustrious kings, a ruler who had risen to power through sheer valour and declared himself the lord paramount of the south. However, his fighting spirit lived on within the Chalukya kingdom.

The Revival and Eventual Fall of the Chalukyas

Thirteen years after Pulakeshin II's death, his son Vikramaditya I formed a coalition with the Pandya and Western Ganga dynasties to recapture Vatapi from the Pallavas. His victory reestablished Chalukya dominance in the Deccan.

The rivalry continued under Vikramaditya I's successors. His son Vinayaditya and grandson Vijayaditya waged further campaigns against the Pallavas. However, it was Vikramaditya II, the son of Vijayaditya, Dantidurga formed an alliance with the Pallavas, isolating the Chalukyas politically and militarily. Ultimately, Kirtivarman II was defeated and killed, marking the end of the once-mighty Chalukya dynasty.

who achieved the most decisive victories, successfully conquering the Pallava capital not once, but twice.

Despite his military success, Vikramaditya II was a magnanimous ruler. Upon capturing Kanchipuram, he refrained from plundering the city and instead showed benevolence toward its citizens. He also respected its historical and cultural monuments. A Kannada inscription on the victory pillar of the Kailasanatha Temple in Kanchipuram commemorates this triumph. Furthermore, to honour their Chalukya victory, the Virupaksha Temple in Pattadakal was constructed mirroring the architectural grandeur of the Kailasanatha Temple.

The Chalukya fascination with Kanchipuram endured, and Vikramaditya II's son, Kirtivarman II, conquered the city for a third time. However, by this period, the Chalukya empire faced a new threat—the Rashtrakutas, former vassals of the Chalukyas, had risen to power under their formidable leader, Dantidurga.

Dantidurga formed an alliance with the Pallavas, isolating the Chalukyas politically and militarily. Ultimately, Kirtivarman II was defeated and killed, marking the end of the once-mighty Chalukya dynasty.

Rules to rule

- **In intense conflicts, Kautilya's four-point strategy— sama, dama, danda and bheda—is the most effective approach**

Pulakeshin II employed this ancient Indian strategic framework throughout his reign. He forged alliances (sama), rewarded allies and loyalists (dama), used military force when needed (danda), and divided enemy camps (bheda), notably turning rebel Govinda against his co-leader Appayika. Lasting success comes from using a blend of diplomacy, reward, punishment and divide-and-rule—not brute force alone. Leaders today must know when to negotiate, when to incentivize, when to act decisively, and when to exploit divisions in opposition.

- **Elephants are not required to defeat elephants; cavalry can do so**
  In the Battle of Narmada, Pulakeshin II did not counter Harshavardhan's elephants with more elephants. He adapted to the terrain, deploying infantry in mountain passes to disable the enemy's advantage. You don't have to mirror the strength of your competitor. Whether in war, business or politics, strategic thinking and adaptability often outmatch sheer power. Use your strengths creatively and turn constraints into opportunities.

13

Narasimhavarman I

The Story

This is the story of one of the most illustrious kings of the Pallava dynasty, Narasimhavarman I, who remained undefeated by any adversary. Not only did he consistently overpower his greatest rivals, the Chalukyas of Vatapi, but he also emerged victorious against other contemporary powers such as the Cholas, Cheras, Kalabhras and Pandyas. From 630 CE to 668 CE, Narasimhavarman I ruled South India with unmatched military prowess, embodying the strength and ferocity of a lion, a quality that justified his name.

Rules to Rule

- A king's greatest strength lies in choosing the right general
- Victory belongs to those who prepare patiently, strike at the right time, and execute flawlessly

The Battle of Pullalur

Narasimhavarman I was the grandson of the Pallava king Simhavishnu, who proudly referred to himself as the 'lion of the earth'. Simhavishnu was a renowned warrior who expanded the Pallava territories northward up to the Kaveri River. His successor, Mahendravarman I, was not just a capable ruler but also a scholar, poet, musician and an exceptional military strategist. Under his reign, the Pallava Empire expanded further up to the Krishna River, bordering the Kadambas and Vishnukundins, both of whom were Pallava allies.

However, the rise of the powerful Chalukya king Pulakeshin II disrupted this expansion. Pulakeshin II, who had already defeated the great northern emperor Harshavardhana of the Pushyabhuti dynasty, began to consider himself the 'Dakshinapatheshwara' (lord

Upon assuming power, Narasimhavarman I strengthened his army, preparing for an eventual showdown with Pulakeshin II.

of the south). Fuelled by his ambition, Pulakeshin II sought to challenge the Pallavas.

He first launched an invasion of Vengi, successfully defeating the Vishnukundin rulers, key allies of the Pallavas. With this victory, he advanced toward Pullalur, a crucial location near the Pallava capital, Kanchipuram.

A fierce battle ensued between the Chalukyas and the Pallavas, both displaying extraordinary resilience. Though Pulakeshin II failed to breach the Pallava defences, he seized the northern territories of the Pallavas. As a result, the Pallava domain was reduced to the Tirupati Hills in the north and Trichinopoly in the south.

However, this was only the beginning of a long and bitter conflict between the two dynasties.

The Battle of Manimangalam: The Turning Point

A few years after the Battle of Pullalur, Mahendravarman I abdicated the throne in favour of his son, Narasimhavarman I, who was determined to reclaim the lost Pallava territories.

His first strategic move was the selection of a young and valiant military commander, Paranjothi, as the general of the Pallava army. Paranjothi was not only a fearless warrior but also a devoted Shaivite, well-versed in military strategy and combat tactics. His courage had already been recognized by Mahendravarman I, who appointed him as a commander in the Pallava forces.

Upon assuming power, Narasimhavarman I strengthened his army, preparing for an eventual showdown with Pulakeshin II.

Pulakeshin II, confident in his previous victories, launched another campaign against Kanchipuram, this time forging alliances with the Chola, Chera and Pandya kings. However, he underestimated the formidable resistance of Narasimhavarman I and the tactical genius of Paranjothi.

At the Battle of Manimangalam, which took place 20 miles from Kanchipuram, the Pallavas delivered a crushing defeat upon the Chalukya army. For the first time, Pulakeshin II's forces suffered a major setback, forcing them to retreat.

The Pallavas' victory at Manimangalam gave them the confidence to march toward the Chalukya capital, Vatapi—an audacious move that no Pallava ruler had ever attempted before.

The Battle of Vatapi: The Ultimate Triumph

Vatapi, the capital of the Chalukya Empire, was one of the most impregnable fortresses of its time. Pulakeshin I, the founder of the Chalukya dynasty, had chosen it for its natural defences—rugged sandstone cliffs protected the city on three sides, and a fortified citadel stood atop a hill with double walls for added

The Chalukya capital fell, and Narasimhavarman I emerged as the undisputed ruler of the South.

security. The city's entrance was adorned with statues of Lord Ganesha and Nandi, invoking divine protection.

When Narasimhavarman I and Paranjothi led the Pallava army toward Vatapi, they had carefully devised a master plan. The Pallavas launched their invasion at the perfect moment—when Pulakeshin II was away, visiting the Ajanta Caves, more than 375 miles from Vatapi. Unaware of the Pallava army's advance, Pulakeshin II was forced to rush back to defend his capital. However, caught off-guard and unprepared, he failed to withstand the Pallava assault.

In the final battle outside the fort of Vatapi, Pulakeshin II was decisively defeated and killed. With this historic victory, the Pallavas completely overturned the balance of power in South India. The Chalukya capital fell, and Narasimhavarman I emerged as the undisputed ruler of the South.

With the fall of Vatapi, Narasimhavarman I not only avenged his father's legacy but also cemented his place as one of the greatest warrior-kings of South India.

Rules to Rule

- **A king's greatest strength lies in choosing the right general**

  A king's fortunes often rest on the shoulders of his generals. Mahendravarman I recognized Paranjothi's courage and brilliance early on, appointing him as a commander. Narasimhavarman I's decision to elevate him to general changed the course of history, leading to the downfall of the Chalukyas. This principle holds true beyond warfare—whether in politics, business or governance, choosing the right leader at the right time can alter the fate of an entire empire or organization.

- **Victory belongs to those who prepare patiently, strike at the right time, and execute flawlessly**
The conquest of Vatapi was not just a show of strength—it was a masterclass in strategy. Narasimhavarman I patiently built his army, struck when Pulakeshin II was away, and relied on Paranjothi's flawless execution to secure victory. In contrast, Pulakeshin II, despite his powerful alliances, failed at Manimangalam because he underestimated his opponent. The lesson is clear: victory demands preparation, perfect timing, and precise execution. There are no shortcuts to success.

14

Dantidurga, Dhruva, Amoghvarsha and Krishna III

The Story

This is the tale of the Rashtrakuta monarchs, who began as local rulers in the modest town of Manyakheta, situated along the banks of the Kagina River. They eventually rose to the pinnacle of power, reigning as emperors over a vast territory stretching from the Ganga-Yamuna doab to the two seas.

The Rashtrakutas achieved this remarkable feat due to their extraordinary military prowess, wisdom in governance, and unparalleled contributions to art and literature. Their astounding accomplishments include the construction of the magnificent Kailasa rock-cut temple, a divine abode of Lord Shiva, which required the transportation of over two lakh tons of rock.

> **Rules to Rule**
>
> - Strategic campaigns supersede mere fame
> - Careful selection of allies and recipients of favour is essential

Dantidurga: The General Who Defeated Arab Invaders

Around 739 CE, the Arab army of Tajiks, led by Al-Hakam of the Umayyad Caliphate, invaded Gujarat, defeating the Gurjars of Lata and capturing Bharuch. Advancing toward Navsari in southern Gujarat, they were met with formidable resistance from the Chalukyas of Navsari, vassals of the Chalukyas of Badami. Under the command of Avanijanashraya Pulakeshin, the Chalukyas halted the Tajik army's advance. Dantidurga, a valiant Rashtrakuta prince, played a crucial role in this battle.

At the time, the Rashtrakutas were vassals of the Chalukyas of Badami in Karnataka. After securing victory over the Arabs, Dantidurga realized that he need not remain subordinate to the Chalukyas. Seeking independence, he defeated the kings of Kosala and With the Pallavas' support—who harboured a long-standing enmity with the Chalukyas—Dantidurga finally defeated Chalukya king Kirtivarman II in 753 CE, establishing Rashtrakuta independence.

Kalinga and occupied Malwa. To solidify his power, he allied with the Pallavas by marrying his daughter Reva to King Nandivarman II. With the Pallavas' support—who harboured a long-standing enmity with the Chalukyas—Dantidurga finally defeated Chalukya king Kirtivarman II in 753 CE, establishing Rashtrakuta independence.

Dhruva Dharvarsha: The Star King of the Rashtrakutas

After Dantidurga's death without an heir, his uncle Krishna I ascended the throne. Krishna I consolidated Rashtrakuta independence, gaining the allegiance of the Eastern Chalukyas of Vengi and defeating the Western Ganga dynasty and the Silaharas of Konkan.

His reign saw the completion of the first phase of the Kailasa Temple, the most extraordinary rock-cut temple in the world, symbolizing Rashtrakuta power. After Krishna I, his son Govind II ascended the throne but was more interested in indulgence than governance. His younger brother Dhruva Dharvarsha took over and elevated the Rashtrakuta empire to new heights.

> Dhruva defeated the Eastern Chalukyas and secured a marriage alliance to cement peace.

Like his cousin Dantidurga, Dhruva sought to expand Rashtrakuta territories. His first target was the king of

Dantidurga, Dhruva, Amoghvarsha and Krishna III ☙ 111

Vengi, who had supported his brother. Dhruva defeated the Eastern Chalukyas and secured a marriage alliance to cement peace. He then subjugated the Western Ganga dynasty, capturing its king Shivamara II but later releasing him on the condition of tribute. When Shivamara refused to comply, Dhruva took decisive military action.

In the north, Dhruva achieved victories against the Gurjara-Pratiharas and the Palas, marking the start of the tripartite struggle for Kannauj. Though he did not secure lasting control over the region, his successes brought him great renown. His successor, Govinda III, would later complete his unfinished task.

Govinda III: The Supreme Conqueror

Govinda III expanded Rashtrakuta power across India. He defeated the Koshalas, the Eastern Chalukyas of Vengi, and the Pallavas, securing Rashtrakuta dominance in South India. Under his reign, even the Cholas, Pandyas and the king of Ceylon accepted Rashtrakuta suzerainty.

> Govinda III's victories established the Rashtrakutas as the most powerful empire in India at the time.

In the north, he overpowered the Gurjara-Pratiharas and the Pala king Dharmapala, completing Dhruva's goal of controlling Kannauj. His victories established the Rashtrakutas as the most powerful empire in India at the time.

On Govinda III's death in 814 CE, he was succeeded by Amoghvarsha, remembered as the Ashoka of the South.

Amoghvarsha: The Ashoka of the South

Amoghvarsha ascended the throne at just 15 years of age. Initially overthrown by relatives, he later regained power with the help of his cousin Karka. His reign was marked by significant achievements, including relocating the capital to Manyakheta in modern-day Karnataka.

Amoghvarsha displayed remarkable military acumen, defeating the Eastern Chalukyas at Vingavalli. He also forged strategic alliances, marrying a Ratta princess to the Eastern Chalukyas. However, when the Chalukyas attacked Rashtrakuta feudatories, he retaliated, killing their prince Vishnuvardhan V.

Amoghvarsha was revered beyond his military prowess. Rulers from Vanga, Anga, Magadha and Malwa respected him for his wisdom and diplomacy. He was also a scholar, authoring *Kavirajmarga*, a seminal work in Kannada literature, and *Prashnottara Ratnamalika* in Sanskrit. Like Chandragupta Maurya, he embraced Jainism and abdicated the throne after a reign of over 60 years.

Krishna III and His Fatal Decisions

Krishna III ascended the throne amidst territorial instability. He sought to restore Rashtrakuta dominance, successfully defeating the Cholas at Takkolam and extracting tribute from the Pandyas, Cheras and the king of Ceylon.

However, his failure to maintain alliances led to the empire's downfall. His strained relations with the Kalachuris allowed the Pratihara king Siyaka to attack Manyakheta. Worse still, Krishna III granted the province of Tardavadi to Tailap II, a move that backfired when Tailap exploited the empire's instability to seize the throne with Kalachuri support.

Krishna III's grandson, Indra IV, attempted to resist but was ultimately defeated. He and his ally, King Marasimha of the Gangas, undertook Sallekhana (a fast unto death), marking the end of the mighty Rashtrakuta empire after two centuries of dominance.

Rules to Rule

- **Strategic campaigns supersede mere fame**
  Military campaigns should prioritize territorial gains over mere recognition. Dhruva Dharvarsha and Govinda III's expeditions to Kannauj brought prestige but lacked lasting control. Today, resource allocation must balance short-term fame with long-term benefits.

- **Careful selection of allies and recipients of favour is essential**
  Krishna III's miscalculations—granting land to Tailap II and weakening ties with the Kalachuris—proved disastrous. Leaders must conduct due diligence when forming alliances and extending favours, ensuring long-term stability.

The Rashtrakutas' story serves as a testament to the impermanence of power. While their empire flourished under visionary rulers, fatal miscalculations eventually led to its demise. The lessons of their rise and fall remain relevant even today.

15

Mayurasharma

The Story

This story begins with a young Brahmin scholar who forsook his education to seek retribution for the humiliation his grandfather endured at the hands of the Pallava kingdom's horsemen. Through unwavering determination and tireless endeavours, he laid the foundation for the Kadamba Empire, which went on to govern the northern Karnataka and Konkan regions for approximately two centuries.

Rules to Rule

- Humiliation can fuel strong resolve
- Strong foundations are essential for endurance and longevity

The Journey from Talagunda to Sri Parvata

Witnessing his elderly and scholarly grandfather being disgraced deeply affected young Mayurasharma, who resolved to seek revenge.

In the Shikaripura taluk of Shimoga district in Karnataka, there exists a village called Talagunda. This village holds the distinction of being one of the earliest *agrahara*s in Karnataka—a place granted by the king to Brahmins, exempt from taxes and possessing several administrative privileges.

In Talagunda lived a Vedic Brahmin scholar named Veerasharma, whose grandson displayed remarkable intelligence and determination. Recognizing his potential, Veerasharma decided to send him to Kanchipuram, a prominent centre of learning during that era.

Accompanied by his grandson, Veerasharma journeyed to Kanchipuram, the capital city of the Pallavas, leaving their home in the capable hands of his son, Bandhusena. However, a distressing incident occurred while both were participating in a sacrificial ceremony. They were subjected to humiliation by Pallava horsemen. Witnessing his elderly and scholarly grandfather being disgraced deeply affected young Mayurasharma, who resolved to seek revenge.

The Talagunda inscription poetically states, 'The hand dextrous in grasping the Kusha grass, fuel and stones, ladle, melted butter, and the oblation vessel, unsheathed a flaming sword, eager to conquer the earth.'

Following this incident, Mayurasharma abandoned his Vedic studies and set out for Sri Parvata (modern-day Srisailam), a dense forested region in the Nallamala hills. In this challenging terrain, he confronted and defeated the Pallava troops known as 'Antharapalas', who guarded their frontiers.

> The Kadamba tree holds significance in Hindu mythology, being associated with Lord Krishna in the Bhagavata Purana, where Radha and Krishna are believed to have engaged in divine love play under its shade.

He then compelled the Banas of Kolar to pay tribute and went on to subdue rulers such as the Traikutas, Abhiras, Pariyatrakas, Shakasthana, Maukharis, Punnatas, and Sendrakas. Despite the Pallavas' efforts to contain him, they ultimately failed and had to acknowledge his suzerainty over a vast region extending from the Amara Ocean to Preharan.

Establishing an Empire Named after a Tree

Mayurasharma named his empire after the Kadamba (*Neolamarckia cadamba*) tree, which grew near his home in Talagunda. The Kadamba is an evergreen tree native to South and Southeast Asia. It holds significance in Hindu mythology, being associated with Lord Krishna in the

Bhagavata Purana, where Radha and Krishna are believed to have engaged in divine love play under its shade.

He chose Banavasi as the capital of his newly established kingdom. This ancient town in Karnataka was encircled by thick forests and the river Varada.

As a king, Mayurasharma aspired to be a *dharmarajan* (a virtuous ruler) and dedicated himself to gaining wisdom as outlined in the Vedas, Puranas and Smritis. His administration was highly organized, featuring key positions such as:

- Pradhan Mantri (Prime Minister)
- Manevergade (Superintendent of Domestic Affairs)
- Tantrapala (Secretary of the King's Council)
- Sarvakaryakarta (Chief Secretary)
- Dharmadhyaksha (Chief Justice)
- Deshamatya (Chief Physician)
- Rahasyadhikrita (Private Secretary to the King)
- Vidyavriddhas (Scholarly Elders)
- Rajjukas (Revenue Officers)
- Lekhakas (Writers and Scribes)

His military followed the concept of *chaturangabala*, comprising infantry, cavalry, elephants and chariots. He also believed in delegating power and involved the crown prince in central administration, preparing him for future leadership. The strong foundation laid by Mayurasharma ensured the Kadamba dynasty endured for more than 200 years.

Kakusthavarma, Mayurasharma's great-grandson, emerged as one of the most remarkable Kadamba rulers. His reign was marked by strategic matrimonial alliances with North Indian dynasties. The renowned poet Kalidasa visited his court under Chandragupta Vikramaditya's instructions to arrange a marriage between Kakusthavarma's daughter and Crown Prince Skandagupta of the Gupta dynasty.

The Kadamba dynasty then fragmented into several minor branches, ruling as feudatories in regions such as Goa, Halasi, Hangal, Vainad, Belur, Bankapura, Bandalike, Chandavar and Jayantipura.

Another daughter, Ajitabhattarika, married Narendrasena of the Vakataka dynasty, and another married King Madhava of the Ganga dynasty. These alliances expanded the Kadamba dynasty's influence across India.

Family Disputes and the Decline of the Empire

After Kakusthavarma, the Kadamba dynasty split into two branches. Shantivarma ruled from Banavasi, while his brother Krishnavarma I governed the Triparvata branch from Devagiri.

Krishnavarma faced continuous aggression from the Pallavas and was eventually killed in battle. His son, Vishnuvarma, then accepted Pallava suzerainty.

Later, Ravivarma of the Banavasi branch revived the dynasty by defeating several rulers. However, his actions intensified internal family feuds.

After his death, his son Harivarma was killed by Krishnavarma II, Vishnuvarma's grandson. Krishnavarma II then reunited the dynasty under one rule.

Despite this unification, he failed to maintain dominance against the rising Chalukya dynasty. The Chalukyas of Badami, once Kadamba vassals, eventually conquered their kingdom.

The Kadamba dynasty then fragmented into several minor branches, ruling as feudatories in regions such as Goa, Halasi, Hangal, Vainad, Belur, Bankapura, Bandalike, Chandavar and Jayantipura. This marked the end of Karnataka's first indigenous kingdom.

Rules to Rule

- **Humiliation can fuel strong resolve**

  History has repeatedly shown that humiliation can ignite determination. Mayurasharma transformed the disgrace he and his grandfather faced at the hands of the Pallavas into an opportunity to carve out his own kingdom. He abandoned his studies, raised an army in the Srisailam forests, and strategically compelled the Pallavas to acknowledge his authority over a vast region.

Sometimes, the sharpest turns in life begin with a moment of hurt. What one does with that moment often shapes the path ahead.

- **Strong foundations are essential for endurance and longevity**
  In every facet of life, a strong foundation is crucial for long-term success. Mayurasharma built his kingdom on principles of wisdom and governance. His administration was well-structured, his military organized under the chaturangabala concept, and his succession planning ensured stability. These efforts cemented the Kadamba dynasty's endurance for over two centuries.

Lasting legacies are rarely the result of chance. Thoughtful planning and quiet resilience often do more than what grand gestures can achieve.

16

Mihira Bhoja

The Story

This is the tale of Mihira Bhoja, the glorious Pratihara king who was a sworn enemy of the Arab invaders. He held sway over North India for an impressive span of 49 years. His extensive empire stretched from the foothills of the Himalayas in the north to the banks of the Narmada River in the south, and from Sindh in the west to Bengal in the east.

Rules to Rule

- Securing the best resources is vital for defence
- Vassals seek independence, so the central power must remain strong and avoid over-reliance

Pratiharas' Conquest for Survival

Before delving into the story of Mihira Bhoja, it is crucial to understand the context in which he assumed the throne of the Pratihara dynasty, a renowned warrior lineage in India. The Pratiharas traced their lineage to Laxman, the younger brother of Lord Rama, who played the role of a *pratihara* or 'doorkeeper' for him. Similarly, the Pratiharas initially served as ministers of defence in the Rashtrakuta court. The first ruler of the Pratihara dynasty was Nagabhatta, who occupied Malwa around 733 CE and established his capital in Ujjain, an ancient city and a significant centre of culture and religion in India.

During Nagabhatta's rule, Ujjain faced a grave threat from Arab invaders who sought not only territorial conquest but also the conversion of the local population to Islam. Prior to their march towards Ujjain, the Arab forces had already defeated Raja Dahir, the last Hindu ruler of Sindh, in the Battle of Aror (Rohri) around 711 CE. Dahir was slain by Mohammad Bin Qasim, the military commander of the Umayyad Caliphate leading the Muslim conquest of Sindh.

Following this conquest, Al Junaid (or Junayd ibn Abd ar-Rahman al-Murri) was appointed as the governor of Sindh by the Umayyad caliph Hisham ibn Abd al-Malik.

Al Junaid continued the Umayyad campaigns against Indian rulers, launching military expeditions deep into India, including Ujjain.

The invading Arab forces succeeded in some regions but failed to subdue Ujjain. King Nagabhatta successfully repelled the large Umayyad armies, which comprised cavalry, infantry, artillery and even a contingent of camels.

After Nagabhatta's reign, his nephew Vatsraja ascended the Pratihara throne. He sought to consolidate the dynasty through extensive conquests, successfully bringing much of present-day Rajasthan under his control. He also launched an ambitious campaign into Eastern Bengal, where he confronted the powerful Pala king Dharmapala. Vatsraja was aided in this effort by Durlabhraj Chahamana, the ruler of the Chahamana dynasty, which was then a vassal of the Pratiharas. As a result, the Pratihara kingdom expanded from the Thar Desert in the west to the frontiers of Bengal in the east.

However, Vatsraja faced a formidable adversary—the Rashtrakutas, who resented their neighbours' territorial ambitions. The Rashtrakuta king Dhruva Dharavarsha led an invasion into Pratihara territories, forcing Vatsraja to retreat

> Rashtrakuta King Dhruva Dharavarsha led an invasion into Pratihara territories, forcing Vatsraja to retreat into the deserts of Rajasthan. Consequently, he shifted his capital to Javalipura (modern-day Jalore, Rajasthan).

into the deserts of Rajasthan. Consequently, he shifted his capital to Javalipura (modern-day Jalore, Rajasthan).

Vatsraja was succeeded by his son Nagabhatta II, who attempted to revive the Pratihara kingdom. He won decisive victories against the rulers of Saindhav and Saurashtra. However, the Rashtrakutas remained a significant threat. The Rashtrakuta king Govind III launched a campaign to crush the Pratihara resurgence, forcing Nagabhatta II to flee the battlefield, leading to the loss of Malwa and Gujarat.

Upon ascending the throne, Mihira Bhoja faced numerous challenges. The Pratihara kingdom had lost control over Gujarat and the Kalanjara Mandala of Madhya Pradesh.

But Nagabhatta II did not concede defeat. After regaining his strength, he launched a counter-campaign, reclaiming Malwa from the Rashtrakutas and defeating the rulers of Kannauj and the Pala kingdom. With Kannauj secured, it was declared the capital of the Pratihara kingdom. Nagabhatta II ruled for over 35 years before passing away.

Nagabhatta II was succeeded by his son Rambhadra, who was an unworthy ruler. He openly indulged in an illicit relationship with his mistress, Kantika, and neglected state affairs. After three years of his rule, his son Mihira Bhoja lost patience and took control of the kingdom by killing his father. Thus, Mihira Bhoja ascended the Pratihara throne.

The Lion King Bhoja

According to the *Skanda Purana*, Mihira Bhoja was a lion in his previous birth. However, before delving into mythology, it is essential to recognize his valiant efforts to defend his people from Arab invaders and restore the glory of the Pratihara dynasty.

> Arab traveller Suleman claimed that the Pratihara king maintained a formidable cavalry and possessed immense wealth from silver and gold mines.

Upon ascending the throne, Mihira Bhoja faced numerous challenges. The Pratihara kingdom had lost control over Gujarat and the Kalanjara Mandala of Madhya Pradesh. To re-establish his dominion, he launched military campaigns in alliance with the Guhila prince Harsha, who acted as his commander-in-chief. With Harsha's assistance, Bhoja successfully reclaimed lost territories and expanded his kingdom to the foothills of the Himalayas.

Mihira Bhoja also campaigned against the Pala kingdom in the east. Initially, he suffered defeat at the hands of Pala king Dharmapala. However, he later allied with Kalchuri ruler Gunambodhideva, enabling him to conquer eastern Uttar Pradesh.

His campaigns in the northwest led to the acquisition of territories on the eastern banks of the Sutlej River. *Rajatarangini*, the historical chronicle by Kalhana, corroborates that Mihira Bhoja captured the Thakkiyakas region in eastern Punjab and extended his control to Kashmir. Arab traveller Suleman claimed that the Pratihara king maintained a formidable cavalry and possessed immense wealth from silver and gold mines.

Despite his successes, Mihira Bhoja suffered a crushing defeat at the hands of Rashtrakuta king Dhruva III, as revealed by the Baghumara (Surat) plate inscription. Nonetheless, Bhoja stationed a strong contingent on his southern front to prevent further Rashtrakuta advances. It took the Rashtrakutas 23 years after Bhoja's abdication in 893 CE to capture Kannauj in 916 CE.

In the tenth century, Arab chronicler Al Masudi of Baghdad referred to Bhoja as King Baura. Suleman praised Mihira Bhoja's strong military, describing his cavalry as one of the finest of the time. Due to his staunch resistance to Islamic conquests, he was recognized as one of the most formidable adversaries of Mohammad's followers.

Interestingly, the *Skanda Purana* contains a mythical tale regarding Bhoja's abdication. The text narrates that in previous births, Bhoja was once a lion, while a deer-faced lady was the daughter of a Vanga king. Due to karmic cycles, they were reborn multiple times, ultimately leading to Bhoja's final birth as a king. Upon hearing this legend, Bhoja chose to abdicate his throne to break free from the cycle of rebirth.

Rules to Rule

- **Securing the best resources is vital for defence**
  The Gurjar-Pratiharas were constantly engaged in multi-front conflicts. Their military prowess was acknowledged by Arab chroniclers, and they maintained a formidable cavalry, sourcing elite horses from Central Asia for their adaptability and endurance.

- **Vassals seek independence, so central power must remain strong and avoid over-reliance**
  The Pratiharas once served as vassals before asserting independence, and later their own vassals broke away. Similarly, the Rashtrakutas declined when attacked by their vassal Tailap II. This history underscores the need for strong central authority to prevent fragmentation.

17

Dharmapala

The Story

This is the story of an unwavering king of Bengal who, for decades, vied for dominance in the Gangetic plain of Kannauj. Despite facing defeats in battles against multiple kings and kingdoms, he never admitted defeat. His indomitable spirit to rule over this most fertile region of India was matched by his commitment to establishing numerous centres of knowledge, wisdom and dharma.

Rules to Rule

- Society cannot sustain chaos for a long time
- Learning centres outlive their founding empires
- Power held by force alone is seldom power that lasts

The Son of an Elected King

Dharmapala was the son of King Gopal, a rare figure in history who was chosen by the people to bring order to Bengal during a time of widespread chaos. According to legend, after a period of anarchy, the people elected a series of kings. Each of them was killed by the Naga queen, the widow of a previous ruler, who consumed them on the night of their election.

> Gopal ruled for over two decades, a testament to his success in stabilizing Bengal.

Gopal, however, proved to be an exception. He eliminated the Naga queen and retained his throne. While the tale seems mythical, it reflects a deeper truth: Gopal's rise likely stemmed from a coalition of chieftains who sought to restore stability after the death of the Gauda king Shashanka and the disorder that followed.

Gopal ruled for over two decades, a testament to his success in stabilizing Bengal. However, historical records of his reign are sparse. No known inscriptions have been attributed to him, possibly because, as an elected leader, he did not feel the need to publicize his achievements. It was his son, Dharmapala, who would later commission inscriptions in stone and copper that shed light on the early Pala dynasty.

The Quest for Wisdom and Learning

Dharmapala ruled for over 35 years, controlling a vast stretch of the fertile Gangetic plain—from Kannauj in present-day Uttar Pradesh to Gangasagar in Bengal. While this territory promised immense wealth, Dharmapala's vision extended beyond conquest and riches. He was deeply committed to the pursuit of knowledge and spiritual growth.

> Somapura Mahavihara, considered the largest Buddhist vihara in the Indian subcontinent, was a remarkable example of Dharmapala's devotion to learning.

One of his first major undertakings was the establishment of Vikramshila Vihara, which featured a two-tier stupa. He later founded Somapura Vihara, marked by its distinctive three-tier stupa. These institutions flourished, hosting over a hundred teachers and more than a thousand students.

Somapura Mahavihara, considered the largest Buddhist vihara in the Indian subcontinent, was a remarkable example of Dharmapala's devotion to learning. Its unique architectural design—with five *garbhagriha*s leading to a central *mandapa*—suggests it was meant to house images of the five Dhyani Buddhas: Vairochana, Akshobhya, Ratnasambhava, Amitabha and Amoghasiddhi. These Buddhas symbolize the five qualities of the Adi-Buddha.

Dharmapala understood that great institutions

> In the eighth century, Kannauj became the centre of a fierce power struggle involving three major dynasties: the Palas, the Gurjara-Pratiharas and the Rashtrakutas.

required great teachers. He extended an invitation to the renowned Buddhist scholar Atisha Dipankar. Atisha spent several years at Vikramshila before moving to Somapura, continuing his work as a revered teacher.

Originally from Vajrayogini village (in present-day Bangladesh), Atisha travelled across Asia to study Buddhist philosophy. He spent 12 years mastering Buddhist teachings in Suvarnabhumi (modern-day Sumatra), then returned to India—likely on Dharmapala's invitation—to serve as a steward at Vikramshila.

According to Tibetan legends, Atisha's fame soon reached Tibet. King Jangchub Ö of Tibet sent an emissary, Nagtso Lotsā, to invite Atisha to help revive Buddhism there. Atisha initially declined. But after consulting Avalokiteshvara and the goddess Tara, he had a prophetic dream and agreed to go. He accepted the journey, even though it meant sacrificing 19 years of his lifespan. His teachings had a profound and lasting impact on Tibetan Buddhism.

The Contest for Kannauj

Dharmapala's focus was not limited to scholarship. He was equally engaged in the power politics of northern India. His reign was marked by repeated efforts to control

Kannauj, despite facing defeats by rival dynasties.

In the eighth century, Kannauj became the centre of a fierce power struggle involving three major dynasties: the Palas, the Gurjara-Pratiharas and the Rashtrakutas. The contest began when the Pratihara ruler Vatsaraja defeated the ruler of Kannauj, Indrayudha, who was then forced to accept Pratihara overlordship.

Despite turbulent contests, Dharmapala ruled until 812 CE. A devout patron of Buddhism, he also revitalized the Nalanda Mahavihara, granting it revenues from 200 villages.

This was a major setback for Dharmapala, who had similar ambitions for Kannauj. The resulting conflict between the Palas and Pratiharas culminated in a battle near Prayag, where Vatsaraja emerged victorious. Dharmapala was forced to retreat to Pataliputra.

However, the ongoing battle attracted the attention of the Rashtrakutas, whose capital was in Manyakheta, Karnataka. Rashtrakuta King Dhruva Dharavarsha marched northward through Malwa, catching the Pratiharas off-guard while they were still engaged with the Palas. Dhruva captured Kannauj, disrupting the existing balance of power.

Dharmapala attempted to reassert his control over Kannauj but was once again defeated. Yet the struggle did not end. After Dhruva's death, the Rashtrakutas became weakened by southern conflicts. Dharmapala seized this opportunity and made a third attempt to capture Kannauj and successfully installed his vassal, Chakrayudha, as its ruler.

According to the Khalimpur copper plate inscription, Dharmapala then convened an imperial court in Kannauj. This grand assembly was attended by rulers from Bhoja, Matsya, Madra, Kuru, Yadu, Yavana, Avanti, Gandhara and Kira. It was a high point in his political career.

But once again, his control was short-lived. The Gurjara-Pratiharas regained strength under Nagabhatta II, who ousted Chakrayudha and defeated Dharmapala in Munger, Bihar.

In a final twist, the Rashtrakutas under Govind III launched another northern campaign—possibly at Dharmapala's invitation. Govind III defeated Nagabhatta II and restored Pala influence in the region. Dharmapala, recognizing the Rashtrakutas' dominance, accepted their suzerainty to prevent further conflict with the Pratiharas.

Despite these turbulent contests, Dharmapala ruled until 812 CE. A devout patron of Buddhism, he also revitalized the Nalanda Mahavihara, granting it revenues from 200 villages. He was succeeded by his son Devapala, who carried the Pala legacy forward by expanding the empire into Odisha and Assam.

Rules to Rule

- **Society cannot sustain chaos for a long time**
  In the political vacuum following King Shashanka's death, Bengal fragmented into competing factions. After a string of short-lived rulers and local unrest, Gopal was chosen—either by election or consensus—to bring order. His emergence reflects a pattern seen throughout history: when instability stretches too long, societies seek a unifying force, even if it means redefining norms of kingship.

- **Learning centres outlive their founding empires**
  Dharmapala's patronage of Vikramshila and Somapura helped establish these as major centres of Buddhist learning, drawing scholars from across Asia. Even after the decline of the Pala dynasty, these viharas continued to shape philosophical and cultural thought for centuries. Empires rise and fall, but institutions rooted in education, inquiry and shared knowledge often carry a legacy far beyond political borders.

- **Power held by force alone is seldom power that lasts**
  The repeated contests for Kannauj—between the Palas, Pratiharas and Rashtrakutas—demonstrated that no single power could hold the region through military strength alone. Dharmapala's setbacks and comebacks were shaped as much by the timing of his alliances and the shifting fortunes of his rivals as by the strength

of his armies. History often favours those who can wait, adapt and strike when the balance of power tips. Influence endured through patience, shifting alliances and strategic timing—an abiding truth across all ages and arenas of leadership.

18

Rajaraja Chola

The Story

There have been rare instances in world history where a prince has relinquished his opportunity to ascend the throne in favour of his own uncle. However, the great Chola king Rajaraja, originally named Arulmozhi Varman, did exactly that. He restrained his ambition and offered the crown to his uncle Madhurantaka, known as Uttama Chola. He continued to serve as a prince, only assuming the throne after his uncle's death. Yet, the long years of waiting did not diminish his aspirations or abilities. In time, he would become one of the most esteemed rulers in Indian history, earning the title 'King of Kings'.

To understand this remarkable choice, we need to delve into the early history of the Later Cholas.

> **Rules to Rule**
>
> - A commander should not lead a battle while seated on an elephant
> - Power should not be assumed in haste

Accession to the Throne often Entails Confrontations

Accession to the throne has rarely proceeded without difficulty. It often involved political manoeuvring, violent confrontations and, at times, bloodshed. These power struggles have shaped the destinies of kingdoms. The Chola dynasty—one of the longest-ruling dynasties in history, covering the period from the third century BCE to the thirteenth century CE—was no exception.

The earliest reference to the Cholas appears in the inscriptions of Mauryan emperor Ashoka. The early Cholas ruled from Uraiyur, now part of Tiruchirapalli. However, the dynasty gained prominence in the mid-ninth century CE under the Later Cholas, particularly during the reign of Parantaka I. Ruling for 48 years, Parantaka I defeated both the Pandyas and the Rashtrakutas.

His accession, however, was not straightforward. King Aditya Chola, Parantaka's father, had two wives—one from the Chera dynasty, and the other, a daughter of Rashtrakuta king Krishna II. The latter's son, Kannara Devan, was expected to inherit the throne. But upon Aditya's death, Parantaka I, the eldest son, was crowned following family tradition. King Krishna II attempted to overturn this by sending an army under Prince Indra III. Though the Rashtrakutas were formidable, Parantaka and his son Rajaditya mounted a strong defence, ultimately repelling the invaders.

Emboldened by this victory, Parantaka sought to consolidate Chola control over Tamil lands. He invaded the Pandya kingdom, captured their capital Madurai, and forced the Pandya king to flee to Sri Lanka. Parantaka's campaign extended there, but the Lankan king Udaya IV took refuge in the sacred mountains of Sripada, forcing Chola forces to withdraw.

The Battle of Takkolam

The rivalry between the Cholas and Rashtrakutas continued. In the final years of Parantaka's reign, Krishna III of the Rashtrakuta dynasty launched another invasion. To counter this, Parantaka dispatched Rajaditya with a large army to Takkolam. The Cholas were supported by the Cheras, while the Rashtrakutas were aided by the Western Gangas, Banas and Vaidumbas.

According to the Atakur inscription, Rajaditya, while seated on an elephant, was struck by a fatal arrow fired by Prince Butuga. His death threw the Chola army into confusion, leading to their defeat. The Rashtrakutas advanced into Chola territory, reaching as far as Rameswaram. The Karhad copper plates of Krishna III, dated 959 CE, record this triumph, including the redistribution of Chola lands to Rashtrakuta supporters.

Appointment of a Poet King

After this major defeat and the tragic loss of Rajaditya, the Cholas regrouped. Parantaka's second son, Gandaraditya, was crowned—albeit reluctantly, as he was more drawn to Tamil literature than warfare. His literary contributions to *Thiruvisaippa* and *Palandu* earned him the reputation of a poet king.

During his reign, Rashtrakuta forces continued occupying Tondaimandalam. Gandaraditya focused on strengthening Chola power in the south and attempted to retain influence over Eelam (Sri Lanka). Initially childless, he later had a son, Madhurantaka Uttama Chola, with his queen Sembiyan Madeviyar. However, when Gandaraditya died in 956 CE, Uttama was still a child, so the throne passed to his uncle Arinjaya, who ruled briefly before being succeeded by his son, Parantaka Chola II (Sundara Chola).

Murder of the Crown Prince

Sundara Chola revived Chola ambitions with help from his son, Crown Prince Aditya II. The prince proved his mettle in the Battle of Chevur, where he beheaded the Pandya king Veerapandiya. However, before he could succeed his father, Aditya was assassinated in a conspiracy.

Historian K.A. Nilakanta Sastri speculated that Uttama Chola—twice bypassed for the throne—may have had a hand in the murder. Another theory attributes it to Pandya assassins. The Udaiyarkudi stone inscriptions name the culprits—Soman, Ravidasan, Parameswaran and Malaiyanooran—who were later punished by Rajaraja Chola I.

The Prince Offered the Throne to His Uncle

After Aditya's assassination and Sundara Chola's death, Arulmozhi Varman was the popular choice for the throne. Yet, in a remarkable show of restraint and political foresight, he declined and offered it instead to his uncle, Madhurantaka Uttama Chola, to prevent further discord within the royal family.

Uttama ruled peacefully for nine years, consolidating

Chola strength against the Rashtrakutas and Pandyas. Upon his death, Arulmozhi Varman finally ascended the throne, adopting the title Rajaraja Chola.

Rise of the King of Kings

When Rajaraja took the throne, the Chola kingdom was modest in size. Determined to expand it, he launched the Battle of Kandalur Salai, defeating the Chera navy and capturing Vizhinjam. He then conquered Madurai and took the title 'Mummudi Chola', signifying rule over the Chola, Pandya and Chera kingdoms.

He invaded Sri Lanka and defeated King Mahinda V, who fled to Rohana. The Thiruvalangadu copper plates claim that Rajaraja surpassed even Rama by crossing the ocean with an army aboard ships.

To counter the Western Chalukyas, Rajaraja forged an alliance with the Eastern Chalukyas, marrying his daughter Kundavai to King Vimaladitya. This provoked the Western Chalukyas, sparking a prolonged conflict. Rajaraja's son, Rajendra, led a massive campaign, razing the Chalukya capital Manyakheta and forcing the enemy to retreat.

> Rajaraja understood that true leadership extended beyond conquest.

The True Measure of Leadership

Rajaraja understood that true leadership extended beyond conquest. He expanded Chola trade networks across Southeast Asia, Arabia and Africa. Naval expeditions brought the Maldives and Malabar coast under Chola control. He also implemented land surveys, reorganized administration into *valanadu*s, and strengthened local governance.

Before his death in 1014, he appointed Rajendra I as co-regent, ensuring a seamless transition of power.

Rules to Rule

- **A commander should not lead a battle while seated on an elephant**

  In the Battle of Takkolam, Prince Rajaditya was struck down by Prince Butuga of the Rashtrakuta dynasty while atop an elephant, making him an easy target. His sudden death led to chaos within the Chola army. While elephants offered strength and visibility, they also exposed leaders to danger. This episode underscores the importance of strategic positioning in leadership—whether in ancient or modern warfare. Commanders must shield their key assets and avoid becoming vulnerable targets.

- **Power should not be assumed in haste**

  Seizing power without consensus or legitimacy can

lead to long-term instability and internal resistance. Rajaraja Chola's decision to wait, rather than pursue the throne immediately, prevented factionalism and built trust. His patience laid the foundation for one of the most stable and glorious reigns in Indian history. Modern leaders can benefit from this example—lasting authority is best earned through patience, unity and principled restraint.

19

Rajendra Chola

The Story

It is the story of the mighty king of South India who embarked on an extensive expedition from Thanjavur in Tamil Nadu with the mission of bringing the sacred waters of the Ganges River to his newly established capital. He successfully navigated along the Eastern Ghats and crossed major rivers such as the Kaveri, Krishna, Godavari and Mahanadi, ultimately reaching the sacred Ganges. All the kings who crossed his path were defeated and subdued.

Rules to Rule

- A commander must taste some battles before leading troops in a war
- One who engages without strategic foresight is likely to face setbacks

The Warrior Son of an Illustrious Father

Rajendra I, the heir apparent of the great Chola king Rajaraja, achieved fame well before assuming the Chola throne. He actively participated in numerous campaigns on behalf of the empire, personally leading the vast Chola army against formidable enemies and displaying unwavering courage on challenging battlegrounds.

The most enduring conflict faced by the Chola army was with the Western Chalukyas, their primary adversaries in South India. These wars were often sparked by disputes over authority concerning their cousins, the Eastern Chalukyas of Vengi. Almost every time the Western Chalukyas instigated conflict, Rajendra I emerged victorious, forcing them to retreat to their capital. As crown prince and later co-regent, Rajendra engaged the Chalukyas on various battlegrounds, including Rattepadi, Banavasi, Raichur, Gulbarga and Manyakheta.

> At the battle of Manyakheta, Rajendra I led a formidable force of 900,000 Chola soldiers and demolished the capital city of the Western Chalukyas, forcing them to shift their capital from Manyakheta to Kalyani.

At the battle of Manyakheta, Rajendra I led a formidable force of 900,000 Chola soldiers and demolished the capital city of the Western Chalukyas, forcing them to shift their capital from Manyakheta to Kalyani. These victories cemented Rajendra's reputation as a brilliant military commander and a rising star in South India, earning him admiration and respect.

He also undertook several campaigns on behalf of his father Rajaraja. These included conquests in Rashtrakuta territory and the region of present-day north-western Karnataka. He assisted in campaigns against Kerala and Andhra Pradesh. When Rajaraja launched a campaign to annex Sri Lanka, Rajendra accompanied the Chola navy and army. He also led the Chola navy in his father's final campaign to conquer the Maldives. Soon after the successful takeover of the Maldives, Rajaraja passed away and Rajendra ascended the throne of the Chola kingdom.

The Northern Expedition of a Southern King

After ascending the throne, Rajendra I annexed the Chera and Pandya kingdoms into the Chola domain. These victories further fuelled his ambitions, prompting him to expand northward into the Gangetic region; a succession conflict within the Eastern Chalukya kingdom added urgency to his expansion.

Rajendra's nephew, Rajaraja Narendra, was appointed to succeed his father Vimaladitya on the Eastern Chalukya throne of Vengi. However, his claim was challenged by his half-brother, Vishnuvardhana Vijayaditya VII, who was backed by the Western Chalukyas and the Kalinga region. Rajaraja Narendra appealed for help, prompting Rajendra I to send a substantial military force under his seasoned general Araiyan Rajarajan, a veteran of the Chalukya-Chola wars. Araiyan Rajarajan defeated Vijayaditya and secured Rajaraja Narendra's place on the throne.

Following this, Rajendra I led a northern expedition along the Eastern Ghats. The primary aim was to punish the rulers of Kalinga for supporting Vijayaditya. Rajendra triumphed over the Kalinga king with support from the Parmar and Kalchuri dynasties. The Chola army went on to defeat Indraratha, the king of Odisha, and Dharmapala, the king of Danda Bhukti, a marshy region between Odisha and Bengal. Finally, they confronted Mahipala I of the Pala dynasty, whose empire extended from Tamralipti in present-day West Bengal to Varanasi in Uttar Pradesh. Mahipala was decisively defeated.

After this resounding success, Rajendra I returned, proudly carrying the sacred water of the Ganges. To commemorate his victory, he established the new capital, Gangaikonda Cholapuram. A grand temple, Gangaikondacholisvara, and a lion-shaped tank, Chola Gangam, devoted to Lord Shiva, were constructed. The sacred waters were poured into this lake, often referred to as Ganga-jalamayam jayasthambham, symbolizing a 'liquid pillar of victory'.

> A grand temple, Gangaikondacholisvara, and a lion-shaped tank, Chola Gangam, devoted to Lord Shiva, were constructed.

The Conquest of the Srivijaya Empire

Contrary to the traditional Chola policy of maintaining friendly relations with the Srivijaya empire of Southeast Asia, Rajendra I launched a maritime assault that led to the downfall of the Sailendra dynasty.

Srivijaya, a Buddhist empire located on Sumatra, controlled crucial trade routes such as the Sunda and Malacca Straits. Arab records describe it as so vast that even the fastest vessel would take two years to navigate all its islands.

While the exact reason for the Chola invasion is unclear, historians believe it may have been prompted by Srivijaya's attempt to disrupt Chola trade with China or by a geopolitical rivalry for influence over neighbouring kingdoms.

The attack was swift and unexpected. While ships from India typically sailed east across the Bay of Bengal into the Malacca Strait, stopping at ports like Lamuri or Kedah, the Chola fleet opted for a bolder route—sailing directly to Sumatra's west coast and striking through the Sunda Strait. Expecting an attack at Malacca, the Srivijaya navy was caught off guard as the Cholas approached from the south. The Cholas captured and plundered Palembang, the Srivijaya capital, and imprisoned King Sang Rama Vijaya Tungga Varman.

The Chola strategy of rapid, surprise attacks left Srivijaya unable to organize a defence or counterattack.

However, the Cholas did not establish direct administration over the conquered cities. They moved from port to port—destroying and plundering Malavu, Tumasik, Pannai and Kadaram.

This event marked the end of Srivijaya's monopoly over maritime trade and affirmed Rajendra I's supremacy in the Indian Ocean, especially along the trade routes to China.

> Rajendra I passed on the courage and strength he inherited from his father, King Rajaraja, to his own son, Rajadhiraja.

Fourteen years after this extraordinary campaign, Rajendra I passed away, leaving behind an empire that was a powerhouse of military might, economic influence and cultural achievement across South and Southeast Asia. Unlike other empires that declined with the death of a strong ruler, Rajendra I passed on the courage and strength he inherited from his father, King Rajaraja, to his own son, Rajadhiraja. This ensured the continued prosperity and prestige of the Chola dynasty, which endured for over two centuries after his death.

Rules to Rule

- **A commander must taste some battles before leading troops in a war**
  King Rajendra didn't earn his fame and glory after ascending the throne; he proved himself to be a great warrior and capable heir while still a prince. Many of

his father's key victories were made possible because Rajendra had already tested himself in real battles. Before taking charge—whether in business, leadership or family legacy—hands-on experience is crucial. No amount of theory or privilege can substitute for the learning that comes from real-world challenges. Future leaders must earn their stripes in the field before they are entrusted with greater responsibility.

- **One who engages without strategic foresight is likely to face setbacks**
  The Srivijaya empire had cordial relations with the Cholas, yet due to a lack of foresight, they failed to anticipate the changing dynamics. Whether it was trade disruption or geopolitical rivalry, they underestimated Rajendra's response. The Chola naval attack was swift and unexpected, leading to the fall of Srivijaya's dominance.

  In any sphere—business, politics or life—entering conflicts without clarity, planning or anticipation can have disastrous consequences. Always assess the long-term impact of your decisions and avoid reactive moves that aren't backed by strategy. Even the most powerful can fall if they act blindly.

Bibliography

Gaurav, Prashant, *Pracheen Bharat*, Rajkamal Prakashan, Delhi, 2009.

Keay, John, *India: A History*, William Collins, Glasgow, 2022.

Majumdar, R.C., *Ancient India*, Motilal Banarsidass, New Delhi, 2017.

Singh, Upinder, *A History of Ancient and Early Medieval India: From the Stone Age to the 12th Century*, Pearson Education, India, Chennai, 2009.

Thapar, Romila, *The Penguin History of Early India: From the Origins to AD 1300*, Penguin India, Gurugram, 2003.